Haunted Houses
of California

by Antoinette May

WIDE WORLD PUBLISHING/TETRA

Front cover illustration: *Winchester Mystery House.*
Courtesy of Winchester Mystery House
525 South Winchester Boulevard
San Jose, California.
Back cover photographs: *The Queen Mary, the Flood Building,
Nick Nocerino and Antoinette May, Ahwahnee, Hotel del
Coronado, Winchester Mystery House, the Grande Colonial in
1928.*

Portions of this book originally appeared in somewhat different
form in *Haunted Houses and Wandering Ghosts.* San Francisco
Examiner Division of the Hearst Corporation. Special Projects.
Copyright © 1990, 1993 by Antoinette May. All rights reserved.
No part of this book may be reproduced in any form or by any
means, or transmitted or translated without written permission of
the publisher.

Third Revised Edition. Updated & Expanded.
4th Printing May 2010.

WIDE WORLD PUBLISHING/ TETRA
P.O. Box 476
San Carlos, CA 94070

Library of Congress Cataloging –in–Publication Data
May, Antoinette.
    Haunted houses of California : a ghostly guide / by Antoinette
May.
        p.   cm.
    Includes bibliographical references.
ISBN 0-933174-91-8 : $10.95
    1. Haunted houses--California.   2. Ghosts--California.
3. California--Description and travel--Guide-books.   I. Title.
BF1472.U6M39   1993
133. 1'09794--dc20
                        90-12758
                          CIP

*To the late Nick Nocerino
and ghost chasers everywhere.*

TABLE OF CONTENTS

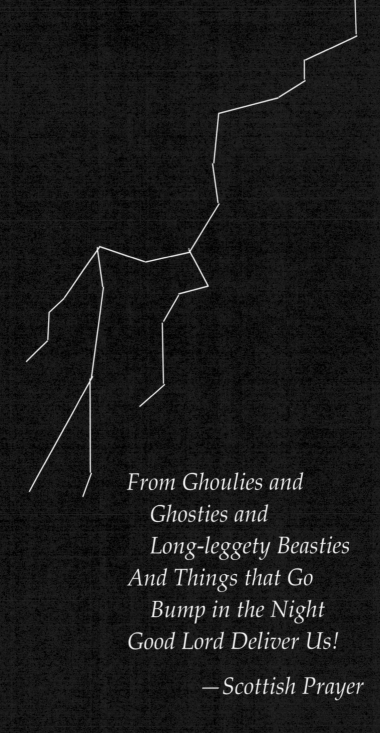

*From Ghoulies and
Ghosties and
Long-leggety Beasties
And Things that Go
Bump in the Night
Good Lord Deliver Us!*

—Scottish Prayer

FOREWARD

Antoinette May and I have known each other for many years. During that time we have spent many pleasant and sometimes harrowing times in haunted houses and places throughout the state. I have known her as a dear and respected friend. More important, I am fully aware of her work as a thorough reporter and researcher. She approaches everything with a needed skepticism, as well as an open mind.

We have spent cold nights and thankless nights in many a forbidding house, such as the Winchester Mystery House or the Toys 'R Us store with the hope of releasing some wounded lost soul.

Antoinette, with some wonderful infused psychic sense of her own, seems to know how to ask the right questions of the medium working, so she can piece the story and events together and not only make it wonderful reading, but an accurate account of what is taking place now and then.

Antoinette's work spans at least two decades that I know of and psychically, I feel she has not even come into her full excellence. With this book and the ones to come, she is certainly achieving it. I love Toni, and you will too. This woman, who has more courage than most, has a pen truly mightier than any sword I've seen.

—Sylvia Browne

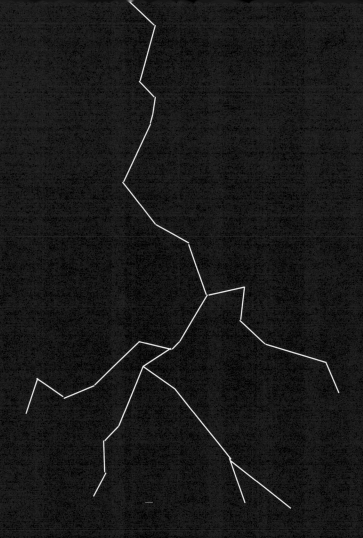

*All houses wherein men
have lived and died
Are haunted houses.*

—Henry Wadsworth Longfellow

INTRODUCTION

I USED TO LIKE GHOST STORIES. THE SCARIER THE BETTER. But always when the story was over, my goose bumps receding, the hair on my head lying flat again, I'd invariably laugh and say, "Naturally no sensible person *believes* in such things.

I used to say that anyway. Now I'm not so sure.

In my years of investigating alleged hauntings, I've discovered that psychically speaking California is loaded and apparently always has been.

The events are commonly connected with a certain space — usually a house. They consist of poltergeist activity — unexplained disturbances such as sounds, smells, the movement of objects or temperature changes — or hallucinatory experiences, such as seeing "ghosts."

The parapsychologists who investigate these stories believe that hauntings and poltergeist phenomena — if verifiable — indicate an untapped energy source and, more importantly, survival of the human soul.

In searching out potential haunts, human investigators may be drawn to Charles Addams Victorians with their long, dark corridors, widow's walks, and dramatic staircases. But the ghosts themselves show a profound indifference to such things.

The ghost, it seems, is concerned with *what* happened to him, not where it happened. In most accounts of hauntings, the spirit comes back to erase, re-enact, avenge or simply brood about some awful event or unfulfilled longing. The spirit of Manuela Girardin, for instance, is said to hover about the room of her ailing grandchildren. Mrs. Girardin fell sick and died while tending the children more than one hundred years ago. Visitors to the historic Stevenson house in Monterey frequently reported glimpsing her ghostly form.

Another lingering spirit is said to be that of Juanita, lynched by a gang of angry Gold Rush miners in retaliation for her having killed a member of their band who had raped her. The tragedy will never be forgotten as long as Juanita returns to haunt the Downieville bridge where she was hanged.

Other spirits seem inclined to continue in more comfortable earthly patterns. What a devoted homemaker Anna Whaley must have been if in death she still returns to her home in San Diego just to check on things!

That California with its riotous history and unresolved conflicts would inspire a legion of restless spirits is not surprising. Even before statehood, Californians talked of a phantom cow, an apparition that wandered Yerba Buena Island, mooing mournfully over the loss of its calf which had been barbecued by pirates. During Gold Rush days Mark Twain wrote of his encounter with the Kearny Street ghost, an apparition that confronted many early San Franciscans.

In December 1871, several thousand curious people flocked to another San Francisco location—the widow Jorgenson's house on Mason Street—where a bodiless head appeared at a second story window. The floating visage manifested itself at random day or night.

Reporters described a sorrowful face with a goatee, droopy mustache and longish, wavy hair. Though Mrs. Jorgenson disagreed, many felt that it resembled her late husband. Eventually the whole window was removed and taken for observation to a judge's office. The face followed. Later both were acquired by Woodward's Gardens, a popular restaurant. After a time the phantom face simply faded away.

Soon after, a group of poker players, gathered at the home of J. J. Hucks, looked up from their game to see another floating face—this time an elderly man with a long, bulbous nose—peering at them through an upper story window. Hucks walked fearlessly to the window and yanked down the shade. Apparently rebuffed, the specter did not return.

Another example of the same phenomenon was investigated by PSI (Psychic Science Investigators), a group of researchers based in Fullerton.

PSI was called in when the visage of a Neanderthal-like man appeared in the mirror of a trailer parked in the Tahoe area. What was it? Where did it come from? Why did it appear? Nobody was quite sure. Members of the research team were able to successfully photograph the image which remains on the mirror today—despite numerous attempts to remove it.

PSI organized in 1973 to investigate psychic phenomena and has since visited literally hundreds of houses, museums and graveyards. Much evidence has been collected including a tape made at the San Juan Capistrano Cemetery of a voice that whispers breathily, "I want to give you my name," Another tape recorded message from a graveyard seance says quite distinctly, "I'm scared."

Though the spirits may be frightened, the researchers definitely are not. Harry Shepherd, a leader of the group, speaks casually of a band of spirits who have seemingly attached themselves to his family. "I see them at night around the bed just as I drop off," he says. There are five of them and if I don't see them all just before dozing off I know that something's wrong. One night I noticed that one was missing and got up to check the house. Sure enough—a gas burner had been left on."

Not long after forming PSI, Chris and Norm Metzner became aware of "Fred," a spectral roommate whose reactions are very much of this world. Using a pasteboard box or card table as a means of demonstrating energy, the spirit responds visibly to the clink of glasses or the presence of a pretty woman. This entity responds to human encouragement and

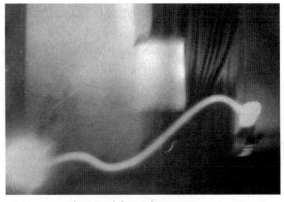

Spirit energy Photograph by Nick Nocerino.

has been known to lift a table completely off the floor in full view of twenty people.

One of the best known psychic investigators in the country was the late F. R. "Nick" Nocerino, who was involved in paranormal research for more than forty years. A gifted medium, Nocerino had the ability to actually photograph spirits. Among the hundreds of pictures he took were blobs, lightning-like bolts or shafts of white light, and actual faces and forms of what appear to be discarnate entities. Some of the images are clear and distinct, while others are vague outlines. In some as yet unexpected way, Nocerino and

Nick Nocerino doing psychometry Photograph by C.J. Marrow.

his associate, Chuck Pelton, were able to act as catalysts between the spirit or energy form and the light-sensitive film.

To take their extraordinary pictures, Nocerino and Pelton used ordinary cameras, Pentax Honeywells with Tri-X 400 ASA film and no light. "We try to forget about the mechanics of picture taking," Nocerino says, "and shut off our conscious minds. What we get in our pictures is sheer energy—spirit energy."

*Nick Nocerino and A. May.*Photograph by C. J. Marrow.

While accompanying Nick on some of his field trips, I observed him take pictures of "things" invisible to the naked eye while at other times his camera was unable to photograph a phantom "light show" seen by many. This paradox seems common to all psychic photographers.

Nocerino responded to thousands of requests for investigations— and sometimes exorcisms—of reportely haunted houses. Photographing the premises was an integral part of the investigation. Packaged film was unsealed on the spot and later developed commercially.

Of course all the ordinary explanations for apparent spirit photography were considered: faulty equipment, double exposure, light leaks or reflections, faulty development, refractions and, naturally the possible delusion of the viewer. Any or all of these could account for the "spirit." After discounting for these possibilities, some pictures remained that could only be explained in supernatural terms.

How might such apparitions—on film or otherwise—be created? The most intriguing explanation is delayed telepathy. Assume that one experiences a severe shock such as witnessing or receiving word of a death. Immediately an image is created which may be intense enough to cause it to be "set" in time at a particular wave length. Possibly years later, an individual whose receiver is tuned to the same wave length is confronted with that image—and a ghost is born.

Judging from the number of individuals reporting spectral contact, one doesn't have to be a professional medium to see a ghost. They attract believer and nonbeliever indiscriminately. What seems to be required is the ability to tune into the electromagnetic field or "vibes." How many may have the ability to do this without even being aware of it?

To be a ghost hunter one needs only a rational outlook, a good memory, a sense of humor and an inquisitive, flexible mind. Basic equipment begins with a notebook and pencil—tape recorders, thermometers, cameras and geiger counters to be acquired as interest increases.

If nothing paranormal occurs while you're visiting the houses described here, you will have lost nothing. As an adventure in historical research, haunted houses have no equal.

As for the phenomena of haunting itself, there's certainly nothing new about it. Ghost stories were popular in Roman times. Pliny wrote about spirits nearly two thousand years ago and there is indication that cave dwellers decorated their walls with pictures of spirits.

In the 16th Century, Emperor Maximillian of Austria called out the army to ensure that there would be no ghosts in the hotels in which he planned to stay. Some two hundred years later Dr. Samuel Johnson observed to his friend and biographer, James Boswell, "It is wonderful that six thousand years have now elapsed since the creation of the world and still it is undecided whether or not there has ever been an instance of the spirit of any person appearing after death. All argument is against it, all belief is for it."

Recently 17,000 persons were queried by the British Society for Psychical Research. In answer to the question, "Have you ever, when believing yourself to be completely awake, had a vivid impression of seeing or being touched by a being or inanimate object, or of hearing a voice which was not due to any physical cause?" nearly 1700, or 10 percent, answered YES.

Perhaps the strongest explanation for the ghost's continued popularity is its implied optimism. A spirit has literally conquered death and come back to prove it. It is both a clue and an invitation to a world beyond our own limited reality, an offer to broaden our awareness to encompass everything and anything that just might be possible.

And who can ignore that kind of challenge?

Antoinette May
Palo Alto, California

Since the original publication of this book the haunted world of California has changed. Many new houses have been added to the original listing. At the same time circumstances have altered at a few locations and they are no longer available for public viewing. We feel that those stories are just too good to omit and continue to share them with you

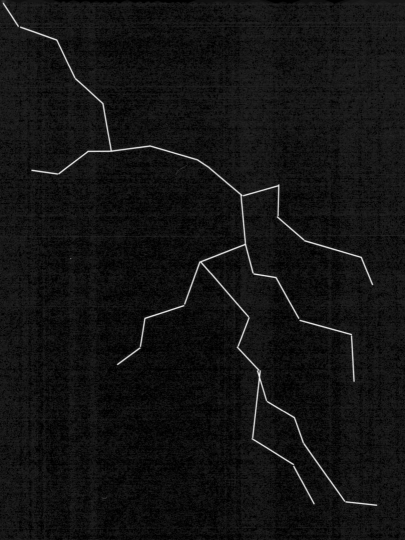

*True love is like ghosts,
which everybody talks about
and few have seen.*

—François Duc de la Rochefoucauld

SAN FRANCISCO

HOTEL UNION SQUARE

THE FLOOD BUILDING

THE PLUSH ROOM

CURRAN THEATRE

WESTIN ST. FRANCIS HOTEL

HASKELL HOUSE

SAN FRANCISCO ART INSTITUTE

MONTANDON TOWNHOUSE

MANSIONS HOTEL & RESTAURANT

THE HAUNTING OF ALCATRAZ

ATHERTON HOUSE

HOTEL UNION SQUARE

THAT SAN FRANCISCO'S RIOTOUS HISTORY AND UNRESOLVED conflicts would inspire restless spirits isn't surprising. Who knows how many specters haunt the historic Hotel Union Square? Concierge Tom Steele says guests like the hotel's accommodations so much that some never check out.

Hotel Union Square

In 2003 a young Scot traveling with his grandmother complained to Steele that a woman ghost appeared to him in Room 207. "She's friendly—too friendly. I was up most of the night closing the bathroom door—then re-closing it. She wanted to come out and wake up my grandmother."

Hotelier Yvonne Lembi-Detert avoids 207. "I turn my back and things appear out of nowhere," she says. "Nothing scary—the last object was a Kleenex—but it still spooked me."

On the other hand, many guests request 207. Some connect the mischievous ghost to Lillian Hellman. A boozer, a lover, a fighter, the volatile playwright was not one to go quietly into the night. She's said to have propositioned a young dinner companion the night before she died—at 79.

Some of Hellman's glamorous and celebrated affair with mystery writer Dashiell Hammett played out at the hotel where Hammett headquartered while writing his noir classics. Hellman's thought to have inspired Nora Charles, co-star of the *Thin Man* series. Jack's Grill across the street is the setting for much of Hammett's *The Maltese Falcon*.

The restaurant and hotel are linked by an underground passage under Ellis Street. Before Prohibition, guests entered the hotel's bar by means of a slide on Powell Street. Lively days—so lively that present day guests report bodies sleeping it off in the hotel hallways. Of course, on closer investigation . . . no one's there.

San Francisco

The Hotel Union Square, 114 Powell St, (415) 391-3000

THE FLOOD BUILDING

MARKET STREET'S MATRIARCH, THE FLOOD BUILDING, MAY be the last place one would expect to see a ghost. Yet building security supervisor Max Canton believes someone or something haunts the halls.

The Flood Building in 1994.

The office building rose phoenix-like from the ashes of the Baldwin Hotel, a destination resort with skating rink and swimming pool that burned to the ground in 1898. Canton says he can hear the cries of men, women and children while patrolling the halls late at night. He speculates that these might be the voices of guests caught in the fire.

Built in 1904 by silver scion James Flood, the classic revival structure, with its high ceilings, marble hallways and iron-railed stairways, is a survivor of another time. Dashiell Hammett, later a famous mystery writer, was a gumshoe at Pinkerton's Detective Agency which occupied offices there during the 1930s.

The flatiron building looms over the cable car turntable and houses—amongst its 226 tenants—the Gap's flagship store. In contrast to the daytime bustle, Canton says things get scary at night. "I feel like something's watching me. I hear 1930s music and, though I wear a blazer and work up quite a sweat walking long halls and climbing stairs, I get a cold chill on the stairwell between the third and fourth floors."

The Flood Building, corner Market and Powell

San Francisco

THE PLUSH ROOM

DURING THE HEIGHT OF PROHIBITION IN THE 1920S, THE owners of the Empire Hotel (now the York Hotel) quietly opened the now renowned Plush Room. San Francisco socialites found their way through a maze of subterranean passageways—some of which still exist—to reach the classy speakeasy where they could sip bootlegged hooch and watch the era's top entertainers perform.

The Plush Room

Many talk of wanting to leave this world doing the things they love best but a piano player known today only as Lester got his wish. The talented and much loved musician dropped dead one night while performing. Well, yes, it really was a show stopper.

Some eighty years later many believe that Lester's show still goes on. Bar manager Tracy Walker says she feels his presence. Brian Morris, a sound and light technician for the club, has seen a shadowy figure and heard the tinkle of an old tune when no one was there to play. No one human, anyway.

The Plush Room at the York Hotel, 940 Sutter St., 415-885-2800

CURRAN THEATRE

HEWLETT TARR HAD EVERY REASON TO BE HAPPY IN THE FALL of 1933. He loved the theater, adored his job at the Curran Theater. Newly engaged, he looked forward to a Thanksgiving wedding. Life seemed perfect that warm October evening as he worked the box office.

Curran Theater

San Francisco

Suddenly a man pressed forward and stuck a gun through the bars. Eddie Anderson, a low-level gangster, had a moll with expensive tastes. "I only wanted to impress her," he said later. Unfortunately, his gun caught under the railing and misfired. Mortally wounded, Tarr fell backwards down a flight of stairs. Friends rushed to his side, but it was too late.

Anderson got away after a wild chase but was caught two weeks later. Tarr's fiancé, Dorothy Reed, appeared every day at the trial. Anderson's fickle floozy, Lorene, refused to acknowledge any connection. Angry headlines demanded retribution:

CURRAN KILLER MUST HANG

Anderson was convicted, hanged, and buried on Boot Hill near San Quentin. That was the end of him, but not of Hewlett Tarr.

According to Tess Collins, the Curran's manager these past twenty years, Tarr still haunts the theater. Again and again patrons report seeing the image of a handsome young man wearing 1930s clothes reflected in the large mirror opposite the entrance.

A psychic once speculated that the Curran may have as many as three hundred ghostly playgoers. And since spirit sightings are common throughout the city, if you look closely, you may spot a few yourself.

Curran Theatre, 445 Geary St., San Francisco 415-551-2000

WESTIN ST. FRANCIS HOTEL

ON APRIL 18TH, 1906, JOHN BARRYMORE, FAMOUS ACTOR and alcoholic, was sleeping one off in room 1221 at the St. Francis Hotel when an earthquake tumbled him out of bed.   The hotel,

Westin St. Francis

San Francisco

now known as the Westin St. Francis, survived that cataclysm only to be shaken to its foundation fifteen years later.

Roscoe "Fatty" Arbuckle, having just completed a film, *The Life of the Party*, was ready for a party of his own. His celebration in Room 1221 culminated in a starlet's mysterious death. Though acquitted of any wrongdoing, the comedian's life and career were ruined.

The same infamous (and most requested) suite—1221—proved even more unlucky for singer Al Jolson, who died while playing poker there in 1950. The Al Jolson Society held a séance in the suite hoping to lure their hero. Though Jolson's spirit was a no-show, there are staff members who believe that both he, Arbuckle and Barrymore haunt Suite 1221.

Just down the hall, an elegant specter in white dress is said to haunt another suite. Howard Mutz, the hotel's former historian, speculates that it might be the spirit of Edith Pope. Mrs. Pope and her husband, George, among the city's social and philanthropic leaders, occupied the St. Francis Suite during the 1930s and '40s. Frequent guests included the World War II admirals Chester Nimitz and William Halsey, who are said to have planned some of their military maneuvers there. If only the walls could speak . . . Perhaps the ghost tries to. Many have seen the lovely apparition.

The Westin St. Francis, 335 Geary St., 397-7000

HASKELL HOUSE

"FIRE! . . . ONE. . . .TWO." IN THE TIME IT TOOK TO SAY THOSE three words, California's most famous duel occurred, the Broderick-Terry affair.

U.S. Senator David C. Broderick had been a New York saloonkeeper and Tammany henchman before coming to gold-rush San Francisco, according to his own accounts, "sick and penniless." Before long he was literally coining money—taking gold dust and turning it into five and ten dollar gold pieces at a handsome profit.

David C. Broderick

With health and finances improved, Broderick studied history, literature and law and was admitted to the bar; then ran for the state senate and became its president. By 1851 he was in absolute control of San Francisco's political machinery—adored by some, detested by others. One historian described Broderick as "the rudest, roughest, most aggressive young man in the area." The young politician made either friends who would die for him or enemies who would—if if was possible—cause him to die.

State Supreme Court Justice David S. Terry was equally pugnacious. When the two met for their fateful duel, he had only recently been released after stabbing a Vigilante officer.

The two men were fiercely divided on the issue of slavery. Terry, a Southerner steeped in the traditions of plantation society, was

San Francisco

determined that California become a slave state. Broderick was equally determined that it would not.

Of all the free states, California had the most stringent laws against blacks. Shortly after achieving statehood, the California legislature enacted a law that virtually made slaves of freed blacks. Under the law a black man or woman could be brought before a magistrate and claimed as a fugitive. Since the seized individual was not permitted to testify, the judge had no alternative but to issue a certificate of ownership to the claimant.

Anyone who gave assistance to a fugitive was liable to a fine of five hundred dollars or imprisonment for two months. Slaves who had been brought to California by their masters before statehood, and had since been freed by a constitutional prohibition of slavery, were held to be fugitives and were liable to arrest although they may have been free for several years. Though it was obvious that the intention was as much to kidnap free blacks as it was to apprehend fugitives, the law was re-enacted year after year.

Outspoken criticism of the practice did little to endear Broderick to the many influential Southerners in government—Terry among them.

There was an angry exchange of words and then a challenge. The two would settle their dispute with a duel. Broderick spent the night prior to the fateful meeting with a close friend, Leonides K. Haskell at his charming bayside cottage near Black Point. It was clear to Haskell that his friend was in no condition to risk his life. He had just completed an exhausting political campaign in which his health had been a problem. The night before the duel he lay on the floor until the early hours of the morning drinking coffee and talking. Haskell said later that Broderick was "fey—all night," that is, a man deeply disturbed.

But in the morning Broderick smiled reassuringly as they climbed into the carriage that would take them to the appointed place, a farm near Lake Merced just over the San Mateo County line.

The behavior of the two parties was in sharp contrast as they met in the early morning sunlight. While Terry's seconds were cool and assured, Broderick's men were uncertain and inexperienced. Haskell partially removed Broderick's cravat and then, overcome with emotion, walked away and stood for a moment wringing his hands in anguish. Sadly he returned at last to finish his task.

Broderick's own confidence had returned and he looked out at the crowd of some eighty spectators who'd gathered, nodding to some.

A toss of a coin determined position and weapons to be used. Terry won and his pistols were produced and loaded. They were of Belgian make, eight-inch barrels which used Derringer-size balls and hair triggers. He had practiced often with them.

The gunsmith who loaded Broderick's pistol warned that the trigger was set too finely; it could be set off merely by a jerk or jar. His objections went unheeded. Broderick's hands changed position repeatedly as he tried to get the feel of the weapon.

The seconds stood back, leaving the principals to face one another from an ominous distance of twenty paces.

"Gentlemen, are you ready?"

"Yes," Terry replied promptly. Broderick hesitated an instant then nodded.

Both men shot between the words "fire" and "two." Broderick's bullet spent itself in the ground about nine feet in front of him. The weapon had fired as he raised it. Terry's bullet struck the senator in the chest, staggering him. For a moment Broderick stood erect, trying to brace himself and then fell backward onto the grass.

San Francisco

For a second the shots echoed in the still morning air. Then a half strangled cry came from the crowd, "That's murder, by God!" A surgeon hurried forward to stem the crimson flow that poured from the wound, while Terry remained erect, still in the classic stance of the duelist.

A wagon was brought and the senator was gently lifted and placed on a mattress within it. The party set off for the Haskell home retracing the route they'd taken just an hour before. Upon arrival Broderick was carried to a second floor bedroom which overlooked the sea. Physicians tended him around the clock. At first their reports were optimistic, then they changed as his condition worsened.

Broderick's sorrowing friends gathered around the bed. For three days their hopes rose and fell. At times Broderick conversed in heavy whispers, his body racked with pain. "They have killed me because I was opposed to extinction of slavery and a corrupt administration," he said at last. Shortly before midnight on September 16, 1857, Broderick lapsed into unconsciousness and at twenty minutes past nine the following morning he died.

In the hue and cry that arose over Broderick's death, the once powerful Southern faction heard its death knell. Broderick dead was a far more powerful man than Broderick living. A heretofore indifferent populace rallied around a martyr's grave. Perhaps Terry, in the thirty years before another man's bullet ended *his* life, had cause to ponder the paradoxical failure of a plan that succeeded.

But many think that death was not the end of the thirty-five-year-old senator. Surely Leonides Haskell must have felt the loss of his friend very keenly. It was in his home that Broderick had first received Terry's challenge, and the two were together constantly until Broderick's death six days later.

When Haskell's son was born a few months later, the child was

The Haskell House. Photograph by Vern Appleby.

named Broderick.   The Haskell family remained in the house with its tragic memories until 1863 when the land was annexed by the military "for defense of San Francisco." This was the opening gun in a lengthy and complicated struggle between the government and Black Point property owners that hasn't been settled yet.   Leonidas Haskell, who, during the Civil War, served as a major on General Fremont's staff, was in Washington still pressing his claim at the time of his death on January 15, 1873.

Over the years a succession of tenants, military officers, have complained that the place was haunted. A man in a long black coat with a top hat has been seen many times pacing back and forth. Could this be Broderick reliving his anguish on the night before the duel? Many people have thought so.

Colonel Cecil Puckett, who lived in the house during the late 1970s, told of a presence in the kitchen. "I feel that something or someone follows me about the house at times," he said, "I even feel that it watches me in the shower."

San Francisco

Subsequent tenants continued to feel a presence.   Capt. Jim Knight, (ret.) a recent MTMC Western Area deputy commander who lived in the house for two years, was certain that the house was haunted. "There's no doubt about it," he stated. "We didn't see or hear anything, but sometimes we'd be in the kitchen and the lights in the dining room would go on by themselves. Or we'd be downstairs and the john in the bathroom upstairs would flush by itself."

More eerie occurrences happened to Capt. Everett Jones, (ret.) who succeeded Knight in Quarters Three and lived there for three and a half years.

"After we moved in we had a couple of parties there and we joked about a ghost being in the house," Jones recalled.   "One Saturday morning after a party, I was in the kitchen putting things away and heard a big crash. Upon investigating, I found that a picture with a picture hook and a nail an inch-and-a-half long had crashed to the floor. It didn't look like the nail had pulled out; it looked like someone had pushed it from behind.

"There was a similar incident later when five pictures fell off the same wall," Knight continued. "And my daughter was sitting on her bed one morning and one of those bolt-on light fixtures fell off without warning.

"There was no earthquake to account for it either," Knight added. "That all happened in the first six months after we moved in—we stopped joking about the ghost after that."

Capt. James. W. Lunn, the last officer to occupy the quarters before Fort Mason was decommissioned, told of going over to the house to check it out before moving in. "One of the painters said that he'd been working on the windows one day and something pushed him right out!"

Later the Lunn family saw plants tip over by themselves and shadows move across empty rooms. "Often I hear footsteps when I'm home alone," he said. "The dog pricks up her ears and runs to look—she hears them too—but we don't see anything.

Sylvia Browne, while investigating the house, saw clairvoyantly a whole mosaic of spirits. First there was a man in a long black coat with a top hat who paced back and forth. Could that have been Broderick?

Then Sylvia described black people hiding in the cellar. "They were hidden there for their own protection, but many of them were frightened and unhappy, uncertain of the future," she explained.

Considering the state of San Francisco politics in the 1850s, this seems highly probable. Surely Haskell, an anti-slavery crony of Broderick's, would have aided fugitives even to the extent of hiding them if necessary in his home.

Those turbulent times have left their imprint on the pretty two-story house where many dramatic events have taken place over the years.

Of course it's haunted.

The historic Haskell House is located at Fort Mason at the foot of Franklin Street in San Francisco.

San Francisco

SAN FRANCISCO ART INSTITUTE

A GROUP OF PROMINENT PSYCHICS HOLD FRUSTRATED creativity to blame for a series of hauntings that have mystified faculty and students at the San Francisco Art Institute.

The Institute is a splendid example of the Spanish Colonial revival architecture popular during the 1920s. The walls are stripped concrete dyed a soft adobe ocre, the roofs red tile. A bell tower rises above the patio in the manner of an early mission.

"There's something strange about the bell tower," students began to whisper almost immediately after the Institute opened its doors on January 15, 1927. But it was twenty years before anything really happened.

Artist Bill Morehouse, retired art professor from Sonoma State College, was in 1947, a night watchman and student at the Institute. To reduce expenses, he decided to sleep in the tower.

He vividly recalls his first night there.. "It was around midnight and I had gone to bed on the third level. I heard the doors opening and closing down below. I'd locked them myself, but I assumed that it was the janitor, so I didn't bother to investigate. I listened to the footsteps climbing to the first level, then to the second and finally to the third.

The door knob turned and the door to my room opened and closed as though someone had entered. It was a large room and well lighted. Inside was a water tank, my bedroll and me. I saw no one but heard footsteps passing through the room, turning, then walking back to the door. The knob turned, the door opened and closed and the footsteps continued up to the observation platform."

That was Morehouse's first encounter with the Art Institute Ghost, but not his last. He tells of another night when he and five friends were partying in the tower. Their laughter came to a sudden halt at the sound of footsteps approaching. "The steps came up, up, up," he says. "Just as they reached the landing, one of us yanked the door open and yelled 'surprise!' We were the ones who were surprised—there was no one there. The steps continued on, going all the way to the top of the tower."

View from the Art Institute tower.

Wally Hedrick, former long-time faculty member, said his most frightening brush with the ghost occurred one night when he was working after midnight. Suddenly, he heard all the tools go on downstairs in the sculpture studio. Hurrying down to investigate, he found no one.

Working as evening registrar during those days artist Hayward King, like many others, also began to believe in the ghost. He remembers closing the school at 10 p. m. "There was no master switch then, so we would walk all around the Institute, turning off lights as we went. Just before going out we'd turn and look back. Often we'd find that one or two lights were on again in the empty building. Of course you could say that we'd missed those lights or there was a short in the electricity. You could say a lot of things. . ."

Once King and Hedrick closed the office together after all the lights had presumably been turned off. As they shut the front door, every light in the building turned on simultaneously.

San Francisco

Morehouse, Hedrick and King believed their ghost to be mischievous but essentially benevolent. The unexplained manifestations that livened their evenings became less and less frequent until the ghost was almost forgotten.

Then in 1968 it returned. This time its appearance was decidedly disturbing.

As a 1.7 million dollar enlargement program began, attention was once more focused on the tower, which was being renovated as a storage facility for the Institute's Art Bank Collection. It seems that a slumbering ghost was awakened.

Several students on the night maintenance shift were convinced that the ghost was not only an evil influence on their own lives but was holding up the construction project. Three of the night crew blamed the spirit for personal disasters that included a serious motorcycle accident, an attack of polio and a tragic family situation.

Another told of studying late at night in the library with his wife. "We heard the sound of chairs being broken behind us, but no one was there," he said. The building program was delayed for many months by a series of costly mistakes and near-fatal accidents.

In response to an outbreak of incidents, a group of psychics gathered for a seance in the Institute tower. With them were several observers, myself included. Frustration was the emotion picked up by all the mediums. "So many artists with such grand designs that never got anywhere. . .so many trying to put their ideas on canvas. . .many projects uncompleted."

San Jose medium Amy Chandler told of seeing a "lost graveyard," a fact later verified by the Institute historian. A cemetery adjacent to the Institute had been obliterated by early 20th Century construction.

A series of pictures taken that evening by the late Nick Nocerino revealed the tower room not as it was but as it had been—with a door and windows that no longer exist. Others taken by Chuck Pelton showed a strange displacement of people within the room—a kind of musical chairs effect. Seance participants were photographed in motion, some fading in and out entirely. In reality none of us moved from our chairs during the two-hour session.

What that means, only the ghost can explain.

Photograph by Chuck Pelton.

The San Francisco Art Institute is located at 800 Chestnut Street.

San Francisco

MONTANDON TOWNHOUSE

"I LAY A CURSE UPON YOU AND UPON THIS HOUSE; I DO NOT forget and I do not forgive; remember that!"

Can evil, angry words carry a power of their own? Is fact truly stranger than fiction?

Pat Montandon certainly has reason to think so. After reading her book, *The Intruders*, one finds it difficult to disagree.

During the 1960s the dazzling blond achieved recognition in San Francisco as hostess of a popular TV show. She gained national fame when listed by *Esquire Magazine* as one of the top hostesses in the country. The image, sustained by many flashbulbs and much newsprint, was "glamorous jet set queen." Here was a woman who seemingly had everything.

Unfortunately "everything" included a haunted house on Lombard Street.

It all began with a party, one more gala star-studded event in a glittering chain. This gathering—in keeping with the astrological renaissance of the late sixties—had a zodiac theme. An added attraction was a Tarot card reader.

The warm, festive mood turned to chill when the seer, piqued by an imagined slight, suddenly turned on Pat and snarled, "I lay a curse upon you. . ."

The words returned to haunt her in the years that followed, fearful years that found the golden butterfly ensnared in a web of dark malevolence. Her house was repeatedly vandalized and fire-ravaged. Her car was smashed several times, her career disrupted, her reputation threatened by ugly accusations, her romances blighted.

Locked windows within the house opened of their own accord. A biting chill defied the normally functioning heating system and totally destroyed the warm ambience of the luxury townhouse. Two close friends who shared the house committed suicide. Repeated threats on Pat's own life forced her to hire round-the-clock guards but they could not protect her from the evil atmosphere that seemed to pervade her very being.

"I don't believe that the Tarot reader caused these things," she has emphasized. "But possibly something in that ugly incident triggered evil forces already hovering about me or about the house itself—once the scene of public hangings.

"Such thoughts would have been inconceivable to me a few years ago," she admits, "but today it would be impossible *not* to believe."

Certainly the most tragic of the circumstances surrounding Pat's residence on crooked Lombard Street was the death of her closest friend and secretary in one of the most mysterious fires ever investigated by the San Francisco Fire Department.

On June 20, 1969 a blaze unaccountably started in the master bedroom where Mary Louise Ward—who was discovered dead in bed after the fire—had been sleeping in Pat's absence. Firemen had difficulty entering the house for the front door was chained and barred from the inside. The possibility that Mary Louise had accidentally started the fire while smoking in bed was ruled out. She didn't smoke. That a guest might have been responsible also seemed unlikely, for the bedroom door was also *locked from the inside.*

Though an autopsy revealed that the victim was dead before the fire, the actual cause of her death was *not* determined. There was

San Francisco

no evidence of heart failure, sedation or drunkenness. Mary Louise's internal organs were in good condition and she had not suffocated. The investigation was finally dropped, the cause of death remaining a mystery.

Pat moved from the besieged townhouse but continued to be haunted by the experience. Concerned for the safety of the new tenants, she enlisted the aid of two mediums, Gerri Patton and the late Nick Nocerino. At her bequest, the two psychic investigators visited the house.

Though Nocerino knew nothing of its history, he was able to pick up psychically not only Pat's traumatic experiences, but also those of previous tenants unknown to her. His impressions were specific, including names and details. Research on Pat's part revealed that the former residents had indeed been involved in a series of tragic events that resulted in divorce, great personal loss and/or suicide.

Photographn by Nick Nocerino.

The strangest incident connected with the investigation involved photographs taken by Nocerino inside the house. These revealed weird light configurations, despite the *absence* of artificial lights (light bulbs, flash bulbs, chandeliers or cut glass, etc.) with their capacity for reflection. Some prints clearly show a woman bending over a drawer with one hand raised as though in surprise at some discovery. The image was not on the negative and there was no one in the room at the time except Nocerino who was taking the pictures. (See photo on page 42.)

In an effort to verify the authenticity of the prints, Montandon arranged to have the negatives printed again under laboratory conditions with five independent witnesses present. The freshness of the chemicals was determined, negatives were brushed with a static free brush, the time of the exposure was recorded and every step of the development process observed by all. Shapes appeared on the prints that were not on the negative and several looked as though light was coming from some unknown source. The same ghostly face and figure of a woman was again clearly visible although no such person had been seen or intentionally photographed in the house. Since the whole roll had been shot there, there seemed no possibility of a double exposure.

Hoping to avert more tragedy, Nocerino performed an exorcism on the house. "It was difficult to bring myself to give validity to such an act," Montandon admitted to me, "and yet, I no longer feel uneasy about the place. Everything now appears to be stable and normal."

One can only hope.

The house, a private residence, is located on San Francisco's "crooked Lombard Street."

San Francisco

MANSIONS HOTEL & HOTEL RESTAURANT

THERE WAS A SAYING IN THE 1880S THAT THOUGH A MAN might make his fortune in the desert, he came to San Francisco to spend it. Richard Craig Chambers was a classic example. The wealth that built the mansion at 2220 Sacramento Street in 1887 had its source in a Utah silver mine. After many failures, he had become one of the richest and most politically powerful men of his time.

A key figure in the development and settlement of the American West, Chambers' life was a saga of migration, struggle, repeated business reverses and finally discovery of a bonanza. At eighteen he'd left his home in Richland County, Ohio and set off across plains and mountains. Reaching Sacramento at the height of the gold rush, he left immediately for the Morman Island diggings on the American River. By 1851, he'd moved to the Upper Feather River Mines in Plumas County, then pushed on to Nevada migrating with the mining frontier as it penetrated the continent eastward from California.

Chambers explored the entire west traveling as far north as Helena, Montana, before settling in the Utah Territory where he became superintendent of Senator George Hearst's Webster and Bully Boy mines. In 1872, the chance discovery of a rich vein of silver proved the turning point of his life, the culmination of more than twenty years of struggle. Immediately setting to work to raise development capital, Chambers assembled a prominent group of backers that included Senator Hearst. A deal was struck, Chambers emerged part owner and superintendent of the mine. The official name was the Ontario, but many called it the "Plumas Asylum". Chambers, remembering his lean days, always managing to find jobs for his less fortunate comrades.

With money, he made money and that money bought power. Chambers founded a newspaper, becoming one of the most powerful political voice in the inter-mountain region. It wasn't enough. San Francisco beckoned. The Sacramento Street showplace was a statement. Next came admittance to the Pacific Union Club in 1892. By 1894, he was listed in *Our Society Blue Book.*

Chambers died in 1901. His wife had preceded him. Since the couple had no children, two nieces inherited the mansion. They soon turned the classic revival structure into two houses by moving the original building to the east side of

Bob Pritikin at the Mansions Hotel.
Photograph by Vern Appleby.

the lot and adding a second half with its own entrance and address. Perhaps the women didn't get along. Maybe the hobby of one, Claudia Chambers, had something to do with it. Claudia adored pigs and raised them as pets.

Then something bizarre and terrible happened. Claudia was killed in a freak accident. The legend has it that she was sawed in half. Today no A series of people lived in the double house after that, but no one stayed long. Once the pride of Pacific Heights, the place had degenerated into a run down rooming house when Bob Pritikin bought it in 1977. A kind of miracle man cut from the same cloth as Chambers, Pritikin, an advertising genius, is the author of *Christ Was An Ad Man* and *Pritikin's Testament.* Transforming the delapidated relic into an elegant hotel and restaurant was the ultimate challenge.

San Francisco

The Mansions Hotel. Photograph by Vern Appleby.

A true Renaissance man, Pritikin has harnessed all his talents—interior designer, magician, art collector, musician and recording artist (piano and musical saw!)—to pull it off.   The Victorian mansions were not so much converted as embellished. Rooms are decorated in crushed velvet, brocade, crystal   and pigs—ceramic pigs, wooden pigs, metal pigs and painted pigs. The new owner is determined to keep Claudia happy.   Though one can only wonder at her reaction to the dinner show which includes renditions of "Moonlight Sawnata" and "The Last Time I Sawed Paris" performed by Pritikin on his saw or to the magic tricks involving a floating head--said to be a likeness of her.

Is it any surprise the two Mansions are said to be haunted?   An obstreperous guest was decked by a heavy door that suddenly came loose from its hinges and fell on him, a toilet seat lid ripped itself loose from steel hinges, a crystal wine glass exploded in the presence of several guests and the diaphanous form of a lady had been seen frequently on the grand staircase.

To determine what exactly is going on, Pritikin called in psychic, Sylvia Browne. "There's a girl here. Her name is Rachel and she's dressed in a turn of the century maid's uniform," Browne told him. "Sometimes people feel her presence. It's like someone brushing against cobwebs. Rachel died at nineteen and remains frozen at that age. It was a traumatic death. She planned to be married but contracted tuberculosis, it came on suddenly Now she's confused and wonders why so many people are invade her world."

Lorraine and Ed Warren, the demonologists who exorcised spirits from the "Amityville Horror," visited the Mansions and felt a heavy concentration of energy is the opulent Josephine Room. "There's an extremely heavy presence here," Lorraine said, "but it isn't negative."

I spent an evening at the Mansions with a group of psychic researchers. We set up our Ouija Board in the Josephine Room and found the spirits extremely responsive to questions of a personal nature. As we were about to quit, the planchette board became extremely agitated, whirling about almost out of control. Identifying itself as J-U-L-I-A, a presence asked that we help her son, Henry Ross, by sending him light. Henry, she explained had committed suicide in the house when he was only twenty-one.

Just then a waiter who'd appeared to remind us that it was past midnight pointed out that the branches of a large potted palm tree were moving briskly. No air currents seemed responsible for the phenomenon.

If ghosts can be "cheered up," this was certainly the place for it. A blithe spirit like Bob Pritikin with his moonshine and magic had a penchant for making things happen, but now the hotel-restaurant is closed. Only Pritikin can tell why, and he isn't talking.

The Mansions is located at 2220 Sacramento Street, San Francisco, CA 94115.

San Francisco

THE HAUNTING OF ALCATRAZ

FOR THOUSANDS OF YEARS ALCATRAZ WAS A BARREN sandstone rock inhabited only by seabirds. In fact, that's how it got its name. Juan Manuel de Ayala, the Spanish explorer who charted San Francisco Bay in 1775 called the place "La Isla de los Alcatraces," (the Island of the Pelicans).

Virtually escape-proof, Alcatraz was ideally suited to be a prison and became a military one in 1859. Among the very first prisoners were American Indians brought in chains and shackles — the survivors of military campaigns against the few remaining native holdouts in the far west.   What a terrifying experience it must have been for them, for the Miwok Indians had long considered the island a haven for evil spirits.

Alcatraz Island. Photograph by A. May.

Recalcitrant—or unlucky—soldiers were also sentenced to Alcatraz beginning in 1907. Their task was to chip rock to build roadways and buildings. The soil needed for foundations and landscaping was brought from nearby Angel Island as vegetation on Alcatraz was almost nonexistent.   By 1912 the army prisoners had completed the largest reinforced concrete structure in the world.   Ironically, the first confined there were the inmates who built it.

The Army transferred Alcatraz to the newly formed Federal Bureau of Prisons in 1933. The following year the government decided that a "super prison" was needed to house the likes of Al Capone, Alvin "Creepy" Karpis, "Machine Gun" Kelly and Robert "Birdman" Stroud. "The Rock" seemed the perfect place to isolate the most troublesome convicts. Surrounded by the cold, swift currents of San Francisco Bay, the natural isolation of the island was reinforced with barbed wire, guard towers and double-barred windows.

Additions were made to the existing prison and then—secretly—a train was sent to each maximum security penitentiary in the country. Without any advance warning — so that word couldn't possibly leak to friends who might arrange an escape—the incorrigibles were loaded on board. The train then headed to San Francisco where it rolled onto a barge headed for Alcatraz.

Alcatraz cell. Photograph by A. May.

Once landed, the celebrity prisoners were marched up the hill to their waiting cells. For a convict like Al Capone who'd actually occupied a luxury suite in Atlanta Penitentiary it must have been a nightmare, but for anyone it was "hard time." Prisoners were surrounded by steel and concrete, their lives dominated by rules and routine. Inmates spent from 16 to 23 hours a day in their individual 5-foot by 9-foot cells.

From the dining room they could look out at San Francisco's world famous skyline. Often they watched sleek ocean liners glide off to exotic ports. All about them were constant reminders of what they were missing. At night in their cells when the wind was right, the convicts could hear the sound of revelers at the St. Francis

San Francisco

Yacht Club only a few miles away. Often they were taunted by women's laughter and each New Year's Eve, they listened while the yachtsmen welcomed in the new year.

Failure to abide by the rules meant confinement in "D" Block, the treatment unit. Here the men were kept in their cells 24 hours a day, seven days a week, leaving only once in seven days for a ten minute shower. Offenders who did not respond were then placed in the "hole," one of four steel boxes where they remained in total darkness.

Suicides and murders were common on the Rock and an escape attempt in May 1946 ended in a bloody riot and siege that cost the lives of three inmates. Though thought to be "escape-proof," there was one attempt which may possibly have succeeded. Three inmates — Frank Morris and two brothers, John and Clarence Anglin — spent months slowly chipping holes through the rear walls in each of their cells. Working at night, they concealed their work with false cardboard grates. The men made model heads of themselves from wire, newspaper, concrete, paint and human hair. Each night these dummy heads were placed in their beds to fool the guards during their head counts.

On June 11, 1962, the three inmates climbed up through the utility corridors and crawled through a ventilator onto the roof, then headed to the north end of the island where they slipped into the water on flotation devices they'd made themselves. The three men were never seen again. Though most believed that they were drowned in the icy waters of the bay, no one really knows. At any rate, they may well have found death more desirable than life on Alcatraz Island.

On March 21, 1963, Attorney General Robert Kennedy officially closed the prison. Expensive to maintain — one guard was required for every three inmates — and deteriorating rapidly from the salt air, the penitentiary no longer seemed practical to maintain.

With the exception of a caretaker, the island remained empty until November 20, 1969. Then, in the early hours before dawn, ninety American Indians quietly boarded two private pleasure boats moored along the Sausalito waterfront and sailed the five miles to Alcatraz. The group

The grounds at Alcatraz. Photograph by A. May.

—college students, some married couples and several children aged two to six—called themselves "Indians of All Tribes." Their purpose was to stake a claim to the island which they believed was theirs by virtue of a forgotten treaty which offered unused government land to Native Americans. They hoped to establish a cultural, educational and spiritual center on the island.

But very soon the Indians discovered the same problem that had caused Kennedy to close the prison. Alcatraz has no natural resources. Everything needed on the island, from water to wood, had to be ferried across the bay. It was a tedious and expensive process.

At first where was much excitement and encouragement. The Indian "invasion" generated publicity. Celebrities such as Jane Fonda, Anthony Quinn, Merv Griffin and Jonathan Winters made trips to the island. Troops of Boy and Girl Scouts sent toys, the United Auto Workers donated a generator. Federal officials sat around cross-legged on blankets laid out in the crumbling cell blocks discussing the social needs of the Indians.

Then twelve-year-old Yvonne Oakes, daughter of one of the activists fell from the the third floor of a cellblock stairwell and

San Francisco

was killed. The rest of the Oakes family left the island and never returned. It was the beginning of the end.

Despite prohibitions enforced by the tribal council, alcohol and drugs were smuggled onto the island. On the night of June 1, 1970 a massive fire illuminated the foggy skies over Alcatraz. Four buildings, including the warden's mansion and the historic lighthouse built in 1854 , were destroyed. Federal officials blamed the Indians, Indians blamed government saboteurs. By now most of the original Indians settlers had left. The rest had begun to fight among themselves.

The end finally came on June 11, 1971 when twenty federal marshals descended on the remaining Indians—six men, four women and five children. They were searched for weapons and taken to Treasure Island under protective custody. The occupation of Alcatraz was officially over.

*   *   *

Today the island is maintained by the Golden Gate National Recreation Area. Each year more than 900,000 visitors tour the crumbling remains of "the Rock."

Some of them see ghosts.

Not surprisingly, much of the phenomena occurs around areas associated with the penitentiary's worst tragedies. One of them is the Block C utility corridor where inmates were killed during the 1946 uprising. A National Park Service watchman reported a strange "clanging" noise coming from the empty corridor which stopped as he opened the door. When he closed the door it began again.

Other employees tell of ghostly voices coming from the hospital wards where maimed and crazed prisoners were frequently confined; and screams, running footsteps and crashing sounds have been heard on Cell Blocks A and B.

The single eeriest spot is said to be Cell 14-D, one of the infamous "holes". It's always cold in 14-D, even when the temperature elsewhere rises to the 70s. Rangers feel an "intensity" in the cell, an emotion strongest in the corner where naked, broken inmates once huddled.

One of the most tragic stories regarding the cell centers around Rufe McCain who was kept in this tiny steel box for three years and two months as a punishment for attempting to escape. Eleven days after being released, McCain stabbed another convict to death. When tried for murder, McCain was acquitted when the jury ruled that the living hell of 14-D had destroyed him—body, mind and spirit.

On September 5, 1984, Rex Norman, a ranger spending a lonely night on the island, was awakened by the sound of a heavy door swinging back and forth in Cell Block C. Upon investigation, Norman could find nothing to account for the disturbance. When the sounds continued on subsequent nights, the park system decided to bring Sylvia Browne into the case.

On September 10, the psychic accompanied by a CBS-TV news team, began her investigation. One of the first areas toured was the prison hospital. As Sylvia was about to enter one of the rooms, she paused in the doorway. "I don't understand this but I see all kinds of cards and notes tacked up on the wall. They're everywhere."

Norman was at her side in an instant, "Do you see anything else?

Sylvia shook her head in bewilderment. "Only the letter S. All I see is an S. I don't know what it means."

Norman was excited. "It could be S for Stroud," he suggested. "Robert Stroud—the famous 'Birdman'—spent ten and a half years in the hospital, in this very room. People think he had birds in his

San Francisco

cell, but that isn't true. He just studied birds. He had hundreds of notes and cards tacked up all around him—things he was learning about birds."

Sylvia turned, moving down the hallway, then entered another room. "Oh, I feel such panic here, such anguish. It's awful, it's almost unbearable. There's something else. . .it's so cold, it's so terribly cold in here."

Norman nodded. "This used to be the therapy room," he explained. "the most violently psychotic prisoners were brought here to be bathed in ice water and wrapped in icy sheets. It seemed to have a calming effect on some of them. Afterwards they would go to sleep."

Sylvia, progressing on to the prison laundry room, had another strong reaction. "There was violence here. I see a man. He's tall, bald, and has tiny little eyes. I'm getting the initial M, but I think they call him 'Butcher.'"

Norman was puzzled. "It could be, I just don't know." But Leon Thompson, an ex-convict who had done time at Alcatraz and had been invited to join them, moved forward and stood beside Sylvia. "I remember a man we used to call Butcher. His name was Malkowitz, Abie Maldowitz, but we called him Butcher. He'd been a hit man with Murder Incorporated before they caught him. Another prisoner killed him right here in the laundry room."

Sylvia felt a wave of pity for the spirit of this prisoner, who, for some unaccountable reason, had chosen to remain in prison even though death had freed him. She decided to hold a seance in the penitentiary dining room; and soon her spirit guide, Francine, was speaking through her.

"What's happening?" Thompson asked eagerly. "Do you see him? Do you see Butcher? What's he doing?"

"He's walking toward us. He's standing now on the other side of our table watching us," Francine, the spirit guide — speaking through Sylvia — explained. The guide, spoke now to the spectre before her, "You don't have to be afraid of us. No one wants to hurt you," she reassured him.

A cell unit at Alcatraz. Photograph by A. May.

"What does he say?" the others wanted to know.

"He says, 'I've heard *that* before.' " Now she addressed Butcher once again: "When I leave this mortal vehicle known as Sylvia Browne, I will return to the other side. Come with me, follow me into the light. You will be much happier there. You will find people who will care for you, people who want to help you."

"What does he say?" Thompson wanted to know.

Francine sighed. "He doesn't believe me. He's going to stay here."

And apparently he has, for the rangers who look after the abandoned   prison continue to report eerie disturbances late at night. The prospect of the Butcher's seemingly eternal sentence to the lonely penitentiary continues to prey on Sylvia's mind. She hopes to be allowed to return once again to perform yet another seance.

Boats to Alcatraz Island depart several times from Fishermen's Wharf in San Francisco. Reservations are advised. Telephone: (415) 546-9400.

San Francisco

ATHERTON HOUSE

WHO RULES THE ROOST AT THE HISTORIC ATHERTON HOUSE? The domineering matriarch? The ineffectual son? The rebellious daughter-in-law? Or the mysterious cat lady?

Can the battle of the sexes transcend the grave?

The Atherton House. Photograph by C.J. Marrow.

Consider the cast of characters. First there's Dominga de Goni Atherton who built the house — now a historical landmark — in 1881. During the lifetime of her millionaire husband, Faxon Dean Atherton, she was condemned by convention to a subservient role. While Faxon spent most of his time tomcatting around San Francisco, she did the family homework — man-aging their country estate. The town of Atherton evolved from their holdings.

Immediately after Faxon's death, Dominga bade a hasty farewell to suburbia and established permanent residence in San Francisco. Construction of an impressive mansion at 1990 California was, in a sense, her declaration of independence.

Then there was Gertrude Atherton, Dominga's audacious daughter-in- law who shocked the haughty Athertons by writing controversial novels. And, finally, there was George who barely had the initiative to tie his own shoelaces.

During the 1880s, Dominga financed George in a series of financial ventures that invariably failed. Then one evening in 1887, the California Street house was the scene of a grand ball honoring visiting Chilean naval officers. "It was a brilliant affair, one for which the new house was admirably suited," Gertrude wrote in her memoirs.

"There were dowagers with acres of whitewashed flesh. . .bulging above corsets. . .hips as large as their bustles; girls in voluminous tulle, all looked me over disapprovingly."

That was because Gertrude had disdained the traditional ball gown, wearing instead a devastating creation of white cashmere which she described as "fitting every part of me like a glove."

Gertrude enjoyed the disapproval of the good ladies of San Francisco, but George did not enjoy *her* disapproval—Gertrude had called him a "mere male, nothing more"—and at the height of the party, he impulsively accepted the Chilean guests' invitation to accompany them back home.

The following day when George showed signs of changing his mind, Gertrude outmaneuvered him. She was not about to allow a few Georgeless months to slip through her fingers. Cleverly she goaded, "If you have any pride, you will stay here in San Francisco and make something of yourself."

He left.

Gertrude got more freedom than she bargained for. After a few nights at sea, George died of a kidney related problem. The captain decided that the San Francisco scion should be shipped home for burial. Hoping to preserve him, the resourceful Chileans placed the body in a barrel of rum and continued on to Tahiti where another captain agreed to take George back to San Francisco. According to legend, the family first learned of his

San Francisco

demise when the cask was delivered to 1990 California, where an unsuspecting butler uncrated his pickled master.

"I had an uneasy feeling that George would haunt me if he could," Gertrude admitted.   She didn't linger in the area, literally taking her inheritance and running.

The mansion had a quick succession of owners.   Then in 1923, Carrie Rousseau remodeled the place into separate apartments, selecting for herself the thirteenth unit—formerly the orchestra chamber of the grand ballroom. Sharing an adjoining apartment — once the banquet hall — were her fifty cats.

Carrie died in 1974 at ninety-three, attended by her feline companions. Human tenants knew little of her but had plenty to say about the spectral inhabitants of the house.   Singer Aurora Booth, when interviewed by San Francisco Chronicle reporter Kevin Wallace, described a rushing wind that roared through her tiny apartment.   Jerrie Landewig, a dental assistant, complained of a rapping on her bedroom door just as she was dropping off to sleep, and told of a former tenant who was frightened out of his tower apartment by filmy apparitions.

These witnesses, who have since moved from the house, were quite certain that George was the spirit causing the excitement. But at a seance, medium Sylvia Browne picked up on three female spirits.   "They just don't like men," she warned the two new owners—both men.

Unaware of the house's history, Sylvia began to pick up psychic impressions of the apparitions which appeared before her.   "One keeps saying, 'This is my   dwelling.'   She seems awfully possessive," Sylvia said.   "She's short, very buxom and highly volatile, a lot of energy there." (Dominga Atherton weighed two hundred pounds and was five feet tall. A native of Chile, she possessed a fiery Latin temperament.)

The next apparition was described as an attractive blond with "very definite likes and dislikes, very independent for her time. She wanted to be liberated and was." (An apt description of Gertrude, if her own writings are to be believed.)

The third apparition, subordinate to the others, was identified as "Carrie."

Hot and cold running spirits made the evening memorable. Room temperatures changed frequently and drastically, keeping the eleven of us who participated in the seance busy putting on and taking off our jackets and sweaters.

Photographs taken that night by the late Nick Nocerino reveal a series of spectral "blobs" that seem to float about the house. Tape recorders picked up a strange moaning sound that no one heard during the seance, but did not pick up the sound of a tinkling bell—the type used to summon servants— which was clearly heard by all.

Spirit photograph at the Atherton House. Photograph byNick Nocerino.

San Francisco

"There is a male spirit here," Sylvia said at last, "but he's so pale and frail. There's nothing to fear from him. "   Then she cautioned, "But bad vibes could come from female ghosts who want things done their way and won't tolerate much male interference."

Does feminism transcend the grave? Sylvia Browne believes that it does and suggests that the Atherton mansion would make a dandy women's resource center.

The Atherton Mansion, once again a private residence, is located at 1900 California, on the corner of Octavia and California Streets, in San Francisco.

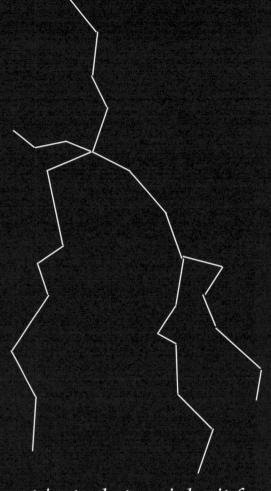

It's not just what we inherit from our
mothers and fathers that haunts us.
It's all kinds of old defunct
theories…beliefs…. I've only to pick up a
newspaper and I seem to see ghosts gliding
between the lines.   —Henrik Ibsen

SAN FRANCISCO BAY AREA

THE GHOST IN THE HAUNTED TOY STORE

TOYS R US HASN'T YET PUT UP A SIGN WARNING, "BEWARE of flying Teddy Bears," but it may well come to that.

Marcie Honey with "talking" doll at Toys R Us. Photo by C.J. Marrow

A toy tipped off the staff that something was wrong, but this was only the beginning of a weird set of circumstances verified by a leading California psychic.

The ghostly games began with a talking doll that couldn't. A customer returned the toy to cashier Margie Honey, complaining that it was defective. Honey tilted the doll this way and that, but no sound would come. Satisfied that nothing could be done, she placed the toy in a carton, intending to return it to the manufacturer. No sooner had she closed the lid than the doll began to cry, "Mama!"

"After this happened a few times it ceased to be funny," Honey recalls. "I began to feel that the doll had a will of its own. Finally I called a clerk and asked him to take the toy away. It cried all the way to the stockroom."

A few nights later, Honey was sitting alone in the employee lounge. Suddenly a large bulletin board secured to the wall began to swing back and forth. Then a stack of papers on top of the refrigerator fluttered to the floor—one by one. There was no fan or ventilator system that could account for this, she says.

Charlie Brown, another Toys R Us employee, had a brush with the supernatural one evening while closing up. He had just locked the door when he heard a banging sound from the inside. Brown returned to the building, unlocked the door and entered—there was no one inside. He closed and locked the door and the banging started once more. The pattern continued several times until he finally gave up and walked away, the frantic pounding echoing in his ears.

Regina Gibson, then a clerk, told of hearing her name called again and again while she was alone in the customer service area and of feeling something running its fingers through her long hair while she was perched on a high ladder stocking shelves.

Judy Jackson, a former store manager, was confronted by a customer who complained, "There's something strange going on in the women's restroom."

Jackson listened in amazement as the customer explained, "I turned off the water faucet, but by the time I reached the door it had turned itself on again. I went back and turned it off, only to have it turn on again. This happened three times and now it's on again."

One evening just before closing time, Bill Peevan, another former employee, carefully stacked a group of shoe skates on a shelf. He was the last one out of the building. The next morning he returned to find them rearranged in an intricate pattern—on the floor.

This and other similar cases of merchandise or equipment being moved during the night is particularly curious. The store—more of a warehouse than a traditional toy shop—is well organized. Everything is kept in an assigned place and the nightly closing follows a regimented pattern.

Once the customers leave, the entire floor is dry mopped. A security man checks to see that everything is accounted for and in

San Francisco Bay Area

place. Then all the employees leave at once with the security agent who locks the door. If any attempt is made to open the door before 9:30 a.m. an elaborate alarm system is triggered automatically notifying the police.

Many of the employees have come to believe that well-secured shelves unaccountably falling, footsteps heard in empty lofts, and lights turning themselves on and off can mean only one thing—a ghost. But of whom—or what?

When Margie Honey and Regina Gibson decided to investigate, their search took them to the Sunnyvale Library. Among the archives was a cryptic note which read, "It is said that the ghost of Martin Murphy is seen on nights of the full moon."

The note has since mysteriously disappeared from the library, but the legend of Martin Murphy persists.

Descended from the kings of Ireland, Murphy, the founding father of the cities of Sunnyvale, Mountain View and Los Altos, carved his own empire in the Santa Clara Valley. One of the very first settlers to reach California, his were the first wheel tracks from the mid section of the western states across the Sierra Mountains. His trail, forged in 1844, would later be the route used by the first transcontinental railroad.

Settling in what would eventually be Sunnyvale, Murphy purchased the 5000-acre Pastoria de las Borregas, a Spanish land grant rancho that stretched from what is now Lawrence Expressway to Mountain View. Within ten years, Murphy's holdings had doubled and his home was the valley's showplace. Described as a "white ship in a golden sea of grain," the Murphy mansion had been shipped in pieces around the Horn and then assembled like sections of a jigsaw puzzle.

On July 18, 1881, Martin and Mary Murphy celebrated their Golden Wedding Anniversary. Concerned lest he slight someone,

Murphy published an open invitation to the entire county in the *San Jose Mercury*. The Board of Supervisors adjourned to attend the affair, as did the judge, jury, witnesses and counsel of a Superior Court trial. They joined an estimated 10,000 guests who partied for three days and nights. Not surprisingly, the gala was described by a San Francisco paper as "the most fabulous social event ever held in California."

Some say the Murphy saga didn't end with Murphy's death in 1884. Many past and present employees of Toys R Us believe that his is a restless spirit still bound to earthly pleasures. They call their resident ghost "Martin" and consider him friendly, if mischievous.

However, this could also be a description of the corporeal Murphy — a man well known for his conviviality and Irish sense of humor. Having been actively involved with the city from the beginning, it's easy to imagine a continuing interest in the present day community.

Murphy was a doting family man who named the city streets for his numerous offspring: Taafee Avenue and Yuba Street for his daughter, Elizabeth Yuba Murphy Taafee (born on the banks of the Yuba River, the first child born to American settlers in California), Mary Avenue and Carroll Street for Mary Ann Murphy Carroll, Helen and Argue Avenues for Helen Murphy Argue, Mathilda, Maude and Beverly Avenues for granddaughters.

But interest in young people extended beyond his own family. Murphy helped found Santa Clara University and the College of Notre Dame at Belmont.

In hopes of meeting "Martin," a group of psychic researchers, including this writer, spent one very long night at Toys R Us.

San Francisco Bay Area

Entering as the last shoppers were ushered out, we observed the regimented closing procedure from the inside. Merchandise was checked and straightened, floors mopped, employees checked out, and the doors locked. We would not be able to leave without triggering the alarm system.

During the night, a giant bop bag set well back on a shelf tumbled to the floor—seemingly of its own volition. Several balls belonging on the shelves on aisle 107 appeared on the floor of aisle 206. Later that night a weighted ball was found in the center of a corridor and was put back on its shelf and barricaded in place by a box. Within an hour the ball was back on the floor again—the box pushed to one side.

The star of the research team was Sylvia Browne, who attempted to psychically "tune in" to the store. To everyone's surprise, she began to describe not Martin Murphy, but a circuit preacher whom she "saw" brooding over an unrequited love.

The preacher's name, she said, was John or Yon Johnson. She saw him clearly pumping water from a spring which appeared to her as bubbling out of a corner of the store. Yon stayed with a family who resided on the property, she explained. He fell in love with one of the daughters, a pretty girl named Elizabeth, but she was scarcely aware of his existence. Elizabeth married someone else; Yon or John remained a bachelor. Browne also spoke of tremendous activity within the area in the years 1881 and 1923.

Flying bob bag. Toys R Us. Photo by C.J. Marrow

It was a long night and at times a scary one as we sat in the darkness listening as Sylvia Browne described the lovelorn preacher whom she believes continues to roam the store which he still sees as a farm and orchard.

Sylvia Browne at Toys R Us.. Photo by C.J. Marrow

The next day the team began the difficult task of trying to validate Browne's psychic findings. Could Sylvia Browne's Elizabeth be Martin Murphy's daughter, Elizabeth Yuba Murphy Taaffee?

1881 was the year of the wedding anniversary party but what of 1923? Newspaper accounts of the time failed to turn up anything of note; but then, for what were we searching?

There was a preacher, we discovered, one John Johnson—known as "Yonny"—who boarded with his parishioners and undoubtedly spent time on the property now occupied by the toy store. Yonny did, indeed, die a bachelor. A spring, now capped, flowed where the building stands. Quite likely, Yonny pumped water there.

Possibly the most startling thing to come out of the toy shop seance was the weird light show of dancing blobs captured on film by Oakland photographer Bill Tidwell. Was the phenomenon caused by lens flare or was this one more supernatural joke?

"Should we call him Martin or Yonny?" Mary Ringo, the store manager, is frequently asked by her staff. Whoever he may be, Mary is quite certain that the ghost exists. Frequently during busy seasons it is necessary for Ringo to stay late in the evening supervising a crew of some nine to twelve staff members. "All of us have heard footsteps walking in the unoccupied floor above us

San Francisco Bay Area

— it is practically a nightly occurrence. And the water faucets—
well, that's really a problem in drought years. They turn on so often that we have to keep checking all the time."

Whatever his identity, Mary and her employees have grown quite

Craig Schriner, Channel 2 photographer, shooting Sylvia Browne while in trance.
Photograph by Bill Tidwell.

fond of their spirit connection.   Their greatest fear is that the
store's upcoming renovation may disturb him.   One thing's
certain, they've no intention of giving up the ghost.

**Toys R Us is located in Sunnyvale on the corner of El Camino
Real and Saratoga-Sunnyvale Road. Telephone: (408) 732-0331**

THE RENGSTORFF HOUSE

RISING IN EERIE SILENCE AMID THE LONELY MARSHLANDS EAST OF Mountain View is the Rengstorff mansion. The ornate structure — a montage of Gothic and Victorian architecture complete with widow's walk and classical columns — has stood vacant since the mid-1960s, a ghostly reminder of a colorful past.

The Rengstorff House prior to restoration. Photograph by C.J. Marrow.

San Francisco Bay Area

The old house, now vandalized and dilapidated, was built in 1887 by Henry Rengstorff, a German immigrant who amassed a fortune farming and shipping grain, and became one of the founding fathers of Mountain View. Six children were born and grew up there in apparent happy prosperity. In 1906, Rengstorff, who had arrived in this country with only four dollars in his pocket, died in the house—a very wealthy man.

Shortly afterward, Perry Askam, the Rengstorff's orphaned grandson, came to live at the family house. Askam grew up to be a successful Broadway singing star, appearing in many popular musicals. In 1945 he and his wife returned to the Rengstorff home. Once again the place was a social mecca. Between concert appearances with the San Francisco Symphony Orchestra, the Askams entertained lavishly. The gala era ended with Askam's death in 1961.

The house was then acquired by the Newhall Development Company and a series of disputes began. Should the place be demolished, relocated or refurbished? For nearly twenty years historians, developers and city politicians have hotly debated the issue, while within the house itself a different sort of energy has made itself felt.

A series of tenants and neighbors reported unexplainable manifestations—the sound of crying late at night, lights that flashed on and off, uncanny cold drafts. During the many vacant periods, passersby have reported seeing a young woman with long hair standing in the upstairs window staring out at the marshland below.

During the early 1960s Max and Mayetta Crump lived in the house. Crump was at that time manager of the Newhall Land and Farming Co., and part of his pay included the right to live in the Rengstorff mansion. For a time the Crumps and their two young sons lived uneventfully in the house, then they began to hear thumping noises on the stairs. Crump bought fly paper which he placed on the steps. Though they continued to hear noises, the fly paper was undisturbed.

During the night Mr. and Mrs. Crump would be awakened by a child crying, but upon investigation they would find their children sound asleep. They decided to move the whole family into one room at night, but the sounds of crying in other parts of the house continued.

Crump then borrowed a rifle specially sighted for night use. Night after night he sat up watching for whatever might appear. Nothing ever did though the noises continued.

During their three year tenancy, the Crumps eliminated the possibility of an animal in the house, for the fly paper was never disturbed nor were there any other traces found. The theory of a human practical joker was also discarded.

Interior view of Rengstorff House prior to restoration.. Photograph by C.J. Marrow.

"Finally I just came to believe that there was something in the house that I couldn't understand," Crump admitted in later years to Robert I. Pack who was investigating the house for the *Times-Tribune.*

Though the Crumps grew accustomed to their unseen housemates, friends did not. Once a couple dropped by when the Crumps were out. While the husband was standing before the front door, the knob turned. His wife could see into the house from a large window at the side.

It was empty.

Adding to the mystery was a set of restraining cuffs which were among the furnishings within the house when the Crumps moved

San Francisco Bay Area

in. No one knows what part they may have played in the long history of the old mansion.

The time came when no one would live in the house. Once a showplace, the windows were boarded up. Whether this was to keep the living out or the dead in nobody was quite certain. What to do with the vacant, frequently vandalized home, was debated. Numerous schemes were formulated over the years.   Among those involved were the three young men convicted of the Chowchilla school bus kidnapping. They had planned to use some of the ransom money to acquire and renovate the house.

In an effort to find out what was behind the strange happenings, medium Sylvia Browne held a seance in the house. Almost immediately she was confronted by the apparition of a hawk-faced man being pushed in a makeshift wheelchair.   One leg had been severed in a farming accident, the other crippled by arthritis. He was bitter, angry. . .

But that wasn't all. Soon a more horrific scene appeared. It was the strangling of another man in an upstairs bedroom. Someone had stolen up behind him with a bell cord. "They want his money, the family wants his money," she explained, "everybody's fighting about money."

Sylvia's experience differs from the original family version, but then *something* must account for the ominous energy that dominates the house.

The Rengstorff House has been moved to Shoreline Park in Mountain View where it has undergone a total renovation to the tune of $1.5 million. Every effort has been made to duplicate the original decor.   The mansion is open to the public for free tours from 11 a.m. until 5 p.m. On Tuesday, Wednesday and Sunday it may be rented for special occasions. Telephone: (650) 903-6073

PENINSULA SCHOOL

A BRIDE DEAD UNDER MYSTERIOUS CIRCUMSTANCES. A grand mansion built at great cost and then abandoned.

The legend begins here and then twists and turns into a dark labyrinth of possibilities. The impressive structure built by San Mateo Country Assemblyman James Coleman in 1880 cost $100,000—a fantastic sum in those

Peninsula School. Photograph by C.J. Marrow.

days. According to one nostalgic story it was to be a gift for his lovely wife, the former Carmelita Nuttall, a woman described by contemporary newspapers as "peerless in beauty and accomplishments."

The mansion was nearing completion when a tragic event occurred that cast a somber shadow over the place for more than a hundred years. Coleman returned from a business trip to the San Francisco hotel suite that he shared with Carmelita. Though it was 5 a. m., the dutiful young wife rose from bed and proceeded to unpack his bags. Somehow, as she was removing a gun from his valise, Carmelita accidentally shot herself.

It's said that the distraught bridegroom never set foot in the Peninsula palace that had only just been completed. The house

San Francisco Bay Area

changed hands several times over the years, no one lingering long. In 1906, a young woman is said to have ended her life there, hurling herself headlong down a steep stairway.

When the founders of the Peninsula School purchased the mansion in 1925, they acquired a resident ghost as well. Almost from the beginning, Carmelita Coleman was a loved (and feared) member of the school community. The romantic tradition of her tenancy has grown with the years, sparked by some very vivid experiences.

Yesterday's Victorian elegance has been replaced by today's space age funk but the legend of Carmelita is still very real. For more than fifty years there have been stories of shimmering lights, unexplained footsteps and pets that refused to enter the building. Generations of children have told of glimpsing the wraithlike figure of a woman dressed in green. Some say the woman herself is green. Once an entire class saw the apparition.

Ken Coale, a former caretaker, remembers quite vividly being awakened at 3 a. m. one summer morning by the sound of footsteps. "I had been sleeping on a couch in the staff room," he recalls. "The footsteps seemed to come from the room just above me on the second floor. I lay there absolutely petrified." Finally Coale forced himself to track the sounds. They grew louder and louder as he climbed the stairs.

Then just as he reached the landing a door opened before him. He entered and the door closed behind him. The room from which the footsteps had seemingly come was empty. The only window was closed. Opening it, Coale looked down. It was a forty foot drop to the ground below and there was no indication of anyone having taken that exit. The house was quiet now. Whoever or whatever had been there was gone.

Mary Anne Collins, a parent of a former Peninsula student and a one- time custodian, felt Carmelita's presence many times but never actually saw her.

Joe Starr and Monique Caine, former teachers at Peninsula, tell of an overnight at the school when some twenty children saw an apparition. Starr described the vision as a green woman who appeared to be transparent. As he attempted to approach the figure it moved backward but remained visible for a full five minutes. Starr asked the children to sketch what they had seen and found that all the drawings were similar—a green woman who seemed to shimmer.

Spirit photo taken Oct 31,1982. Photograph by C.J. Marrow.

Starr encountered the apparition another night. This time the green lady confronted him in a black hallway when he was all alone. He flipped the light switch, but nothing happened. Man and ghost stared at one another for a few very long moments. Then the vision simply disappeared.

Many of the students are quite blasé about their ghost. "I see it all the time," Shawn Kelman told an interviewer. "She's green." Panos Koutsoyannis told of "running through it"—to the amazement of a group of playmates.

Barney Young, former director of the school, believes the ghost to be a benevolent one, pointing out that no one has ever been hurt by it. "The green lady has a way of taking hold of us. Kids may start out by being rather skeptical. 'I don't believe in that kind of stuff,' a newcomer will say. I always think to myself, 'Just ask him about the ghost in another year, after he's been here at night some

San Francisco Bay Area

time. That's enough to make a believer of anyone.' Often kids will say, 'Come quick! There's the ghost!' Teachers think they're being put on until they see it too."

Anna Mary Peck, who researched the Peninsula School for a study in folklore in 1973, found mystical significance in the very greenness of the ghost. In ancient heraldry, green symbolized eternal life, youth and hope —very appropriate for an old school ghost.

A decorator's nightmare, but a child's delight, the Peninsula School was the site of the movie, *Escape from Witch Mountain*. If houses can be typecast—this one was a natural.

At last a seance was held at the school. In the presence of some fifty people, a voice speaking through the San Francisco medium Macelle Brown introduced herself as the original owner; and related a heretofore untold tale of an unhappy marriage, a lover, a very jealous husband and a murder—her own.

Then, to everyone's surprise, another ghost "came through" claiming to be Carmelita's father, R.R. Nuttall, but dismissing her story as "hogwash."

"Why shouldn't I be here?" he demanded to know. "It was my money that built the place, not Coleman's." Nuttall then explained that he visits the school from time to time to note the modern improvements and watch the students. He enjoys children, likes progress, has no messages and wishes no one ill.

What really happened?

How will we ever know when even the ghosts themselves can't get their stories straight.

The Peninsula School is located at Peninsula Way in Menlo Park.Telephone: (650) 325-1584

KOHL MANSION

NONE DOUBTED THAT IT WAS A FATAL ATTRACTION, THE
dangerous liaison of its day.

The Kohl Mansion. Photograp by Vern Appleby.

Whatever leading citizens said publicly, most certainly their
private view was that the upstairs, downstairs relationship between
the married socialite, Frederick Kohl, and his mother's maid, Adele
Verge, had clearly gone too far.

Born in 1863, Frederick Kohl, son of the Alaska Commercial
Company shipping magnate, grew up on the Kohl estate, now
Central Park in San Mateo. Young "Freddie" hunted with the
hounds and rode polo ponies on the Peninsula, site of the elegant

summer estates then popular with wealthy San Franciscans. At his father's death in 1893, he inherited a multi-million dollar estate. Dashing Freddie was considered a catch. His choice was the lovely Elizabeth "Bessie" Goody, an aristocratic Washingtonian renowned for singing talent as well as beauty.

It was a marriage made in heaven—at least that's what the bridegroom said, and who could doubt him. In 1909, the couple sailed to Europe with Kohl's mother who, while there, engaged a maid, Adele Verge. Green-eyed, raven haired, Adele was high strung, almost haughty. She was French and came with the highest recommendations from the very finest families.

Problems developed months later on another family vacation, this one to the Glenwood Inn in Riverside. While there, the high handed Adele got into an argument with a chauffeur and not only slapped him but spat in his face. Fred Miller, manager of the inn, had her arrested. "She belongs in an asylum," he told the police. The court disagreed. Adele was a bit on the temperamental side, but surely not deranged. She went free.

Kohl suggested a return to France, offering to pay her way. Refusing, Adele followed them north. In San Francisco, she filed suit against both her former employer and Miller charging malicious arrest and harassment.

On the afternoon of June 8, 1911, Adele Verge—according to newspaper accounts--listened, "an unnatural glare in her hard and blazing eyes," as the judge ruled against her. She would receive nothing.

Rushing from the room, Adele was waiting by the elevator when Kohl emerged on the first floor. Drawing a derringer from her handbag, she fired point blank at him. "I knew it would come to this," he muttered unaccountably slumping to the floor. Adele turned and fled, but was apprehended while walking aimlessly along Market Street. "I don't know why I did it," the former maid sobbed to a French Catholic priest with whom she spent the night praying for Kohl's recovery.

Kohl lived, but the bullet, lodged dangerously close to his heart, remained imbedded there for the rest of his life. When the victim refused to press charges, no trial was held and the would-be murderess was deported to France and confined to an asylum.

Seemingly, Bessie and Frederick put their troubles behind them. The following year they began work on an elaborate Tudor style mansion on 40 acres of land in Burlingame, then a small, conservative town with one doctor, newly paved streets and a streetcar that climbed Hillside Drive, ending just one block from the estate. On Christmas 1914, the Kohls opened the manor doors for their first party and continued to entertain lavishly for two years. The rosebrick mansion towered over an estate that included a tennis court, greenhouses, a rose garden, a large carriage house and a 150,000 gallon reservoir. The mansion alone cost $424,000. All this was not quite enough, it would seem, to dispel memories of Adele.

In 1916, the couple separated—Freddie suspected Bessie of seeing other men. She took her singing talents to Europe, entertaining World War I troops while Kohl did his best to console himself with the glamorous Marion Louderback Lord. Whatever happiness they found was shortlived, the bullet in his chest was a constant source of pain; and, as though that weren't enough, Kohl began to suffer debilitating anxiety. His troubles with Adele were far from over. Upon her release from the asylum, she'd written him threatening to finish the job.

In 1920, Adele wrote first from Quebec, then British Columbia—she was coming closer and closer. Kohl's attorneys urged the Canadian authorities to arrest Adele and have her extradited to California to face trial. She was arrested, but extradition refused. Released at last, Adele disappeared. Kohl, certain that she was on her way to kill him, fled with Marion to the Del Monte Lodge in Monterey.

On November 23, 1921, he breakfasted alone in his suite. At 10 a.m. a single shot was heard. Kohl was found, still seated at the table, a .38 caliber revolver clutched in his hand. The bullet had passed through his skull, lodging in the wall.

One way or another, it appeared that Adele Verge had gotten her revenge.

But was this the end of Freddie? Hardly. The story had barely begun. The Kohl estate was bequeathed to Marion Lord, who rented it to United Artists for production of the the most ambitious movie of the era, *Little Lord Fauntleroy*. The film capped the career of "America's Sweetheart," Mary Pickford, who played both Fauntleroy and his mother. You either liked Pickford or you didn't. Those who didn't must have been thrown into diabetic comas from the abundance of so much unadulterated sweetness.

Nevertheless, the effect did manage to change the image of the Kohl mansion. Pickford in her black velvet suit, lacy white collar and shoulder length curls did much to dispel both the rumors of the ill fated affair and the naughty reality of the scandalous Marion Lord.

The Sisters of Mercy now thought it appropriate for a nunnery. The 63- room mansion was acquired by the order, which totally transformed its ambience. Theirs was a regulated life. Novices abstained from unnecessary conversation and were constantly warned to guard against familiarity with anyone. They were never to raise their eyes immodestly. Visits to town were forbidden.

Tradition had it that if a girl took even a single step off the grounds she would have to begin her novitiate anew.

It's difficult to imagine that such behavior would adversely impact outsiders, but incredibly it did. Beginning in 1924, members of the Ku Klux Klan, in their guise of protectors of "truth and justice," began to terrorize the sisters. There was a series of letters and phone calls which culminated one night in 1925 with the arrival of white hooded thugs who drove their cars, horns honking, around and around the convent before setting a 40 foot cross ablaze on a nearby hill.

As though threatened violence from without wasn't bad enough, the women gradually became aware of a mysterious presence within the mansion. One novice slept in a fourth floor dormitory room. Often she awakened to find a white powder in the "strangest places"—the   sisters' shoes, on the stairs, and on the tops of the drapes—twenty feet above the floor. Sisters sat up all night hoping to apprehend the intruder, all to no avail. There were footsteps, unaccountable footsteps--and that was all.

Visitors sleeping in the third floor guest room reported hearing the sound of invisible gravel unexplainably thrown at the window. Then there were limping footsteps coming from Freddie's billiard room down the long corridor. Freddie had had a limp, someone recalled. But Freddie was dead.

At first the nuns suspected a few high spirited girls of playing upon the superstitions of the others, but after some persistent interrogation this theory was abandoned. The spirits involved were of a different and seemingly far more dangerous derivation. Exorcism seemed the only solution.

Priests were called in to liberate the convent from the mysterious force that seemingly permeated the place. Two masses were said.

San Francisco Bay Area

The fathers led a procession of fifty nuns, blessing every room and closet in the house and sprinkling holy water throughout the gardens. Did it work? Apparently not, for in 1931 the nunnery was closed.

Freddie's a stubborn case, it seems. The visions, the eerie sounds in the night still persist. Present day staff members complain about the elevator that goes up and down by itself and a professional who came in to clean up after a particularly rowdy Halloween party felt the house "vibrate" for hours.

But now it would appear that Freddie has undergone a personality change. Perhaps not the happiest of men in life—surely not the luckiest—today he appears in his element. The Kohl Mansion has evolved into a private high school, concert and reception hall with Freddie assuming a kind of public relations role. No longer the guilty, anxiety ridden victim of an unfortunate association, the "new" Freddie is something of a social butterfly and patron of the arts. Considering the lively interest sparked by his long ago legend and present day antics, Freddie is one ghost who is very much a social asset.

The Kohl Mansion is located at 2750 Adeline Drive, Burlingame, CA 94010. Telephone (650) 343-3631.

WHEELER OFFICE

WEBSTER DEFINES THE POLTERGEIST AS "A MISCHIEVOUS GHOST held to be responsible for unexplained noises."

This prosaic definition hardly describes the pandemonium that has terrorized homeowners, theater goers, patrons of bars, hotels, bakeries and even used car lots. It doesn't mention the variety of smells that have pleased or sickened witnesses and can't begin to convey the horror of finding oneself choked by unseen hands or the sight of sudden bursts of flame, flying knives or falling stones.

Students of the phenomena have attempted to explain poltergeists in one of three ways: earthbound spirits, energy caused by suppressed frustrations, or the devil.

It was a very bad day at the office for members of George H. Wheeler's court reporting firm, who finally gave up the business as usual pretense on June 16, 1964 and called police to their office on Franklin Street in Oakland. It was fervently hoped by all that the long arm of the law could reach into the realm of the supernatural.

After several weeks of bedlam that defied explanation, they had come to believe that their otherwise ordinary office had been targeted by poltergeist forces. Whether earthbound spirits, suppressed frustrations or the devil—they wanted out.

What happened still remains a mystery to those involved, but Dr. Arthur Hastings, a University of California parapsychologist, developed some very provocative theories.

When asked to investigate the case, he soon discovered a strange set of circumstances. Early in January a twenty-year-old man had

San Francisco Bay Area

been employed by the firm as a typist. He was apparently liked by all, but treated somewhat as a child. "There's no doubt that he was low man on the totem pole and knew it," Hastings explained to me.

"A few weeks later phones began to ring for no reason. Once answered, there was no one on the line. The ringing would then begin again so quickly that there was no time for an outside prankster to dial, wait for an answer, hang up and dial again," Hastings says. "This began in February. By March the calls had increased so that it became impossible for anyone to call the office because the lines were constantly busy, yet no one was calling out.

"Every telephone had to be replaced, although the phone company was positive that each was in perfect working order. Once this had been accomplished, the mysterious calls stopped."

Unfortunately this was only the beginning. All at once typewriter springs began to break. As fast as Joseph Morrow, the typewriter repairman, would fix one machine, another would suddenly break. Mystified, Morrow could find no cause for such an occurrence. The machines were mostly new, had always been serviced regularly and until that time had worked perfectly.

James Ambrosia, the city electrical building inspector, was called and gave the office a thorough going over. He could find nothing wrong— electrically speaking.

Next, coffee cups began to blow up and bulky six-foot cabinets tipped over for no apparent reason. Framed plaques and pictures flew off the wall and a ceramic vase shot seven feet from a closet shelf across the room before crashing to the floor.

By this time everyone in the office was certain that the young employee was the culprit, for the disturbances invariably occurred in his presence. At the same time, they were all in agreement that he was doing nothing manually to cause them.

Another strong indication of his guilt became apparent when the young man would leave the office, located on the third floor of a large building, to visit acquaintances on other floors. The phenomena went with him, occurring everywhere he went. Meanwhile back in the court reporting office, peace and quiet prevailed.

"Surprisingly, there was very little animosity directed toward the man," Hastings says. "Though all agreed that he was causing the problems that were literally destroying the office and most accepted the theory of pent up hostilities somehow triggering the violence, they remained tolerant. It was as though they, themselves, somehow assumed a portion of the responsibility. It was a kind of family situation with all the implicit characteristics of conflict, punishment and forgiveness inherent in such a relationship."

The young man was allowed to take his typing home. Immediately the troubles stopped. When he returned, they began again. The pattern continued until the inevitable publicity brought the police into the case.

"After hours of questioning, the man confessed and was released almost immediately," Hastings says. "No one — probably not even the police—took the confession seriously. To have tipped over a large filing cabinet in the presence of six people without their awareness would have been difficult in the extreme. Yet somehow the arrest and public atonement satisfied some need. Though his job remained open to him, the young man insisted upon quitting. He has not been heard from again. It is unlikely that he will be.

What could he possibly do for an encore?

The Wheeler Office was located on Franklin St. in Oakland.

San Francisco Bay Area

BLACK DIAMOND MINE PRESERVE

A PAIR OF LOVERS GOT A THRILL THEY HADN'T BARGAINED FOR when they stopped to park by the Rose Hill graveyard south of Pittsburgh.

The isolated little coal miners' cemetery in the Black Diamond Mines Regional Preserve seemed ideally suited to total privacy. But the romance cooled to chills when they looked up and saw a "glowing lady" gliding above the headstones in their direction. The woman cowered under the dashboard while the man fled down the hillside, finally stumbling ignominiously into a stream.

The apparition faded, but not the stories about the area.   The lonely, windswept burial ground is flanked by the remains of two ghost towns, Nortonville and Somersville, to which—during the heyday of the Black Diamond Mine—hundreds of men and boys came from Wales hoping for a brighter future in the golden land. Their excitement was brief, their dreams short lived; for the coal proved of poor quality and the mine petered out.

Little remains of the once bustling era but the cemetery guarded by five stately cypress trees rising sentinel-like against the amber hillside.   Many of the pioneers, including Noah Norton, are buried there, a silent testimony to mine disasters and black lung, of women who died in childbirth and children lost to smallpox and typhoid.

Unfortunately they have not been allowed to rest in peace. Graves have been excavated by looters and gravestones—some lettered in Welsh—have been stolen.

According to the late psychic Nick Nocerino, this wanton desecration is what has caused the eerie phenomena that surrounds the graveyard where ghostly laughter, cries and the tolling of bells have frequently been reported.

Nocerino visited the cemetery late at night, making contact with the spirits who have voiced their displeasure. In a newspaper article, he urged that the tombstones be returned. Some were dumped unceremoniously on his front yard late at night. The stones were returned to the cemetery, but many are still missing. Though more than 100 known grave sites have been exorcised, disturbances continue.

Spirit energy photographed at night above Rose Hill Cemetery by Nick Nocerino.

Perhaps the living may still make amends to the angry dead. Peace may be returned to these unhappy spirits when their property—mute testimony to their mortal existence—is finally restored.

To reach the graveyard, take Highway 4 out of Concord east to the Loveridge Road exit, head south, then turn left at Buchanan. Turn right on Somersville and drive to the end at the preserve's parking lot where the trail to Rose Hill Cemetery begins.

San Francisco Bay Area

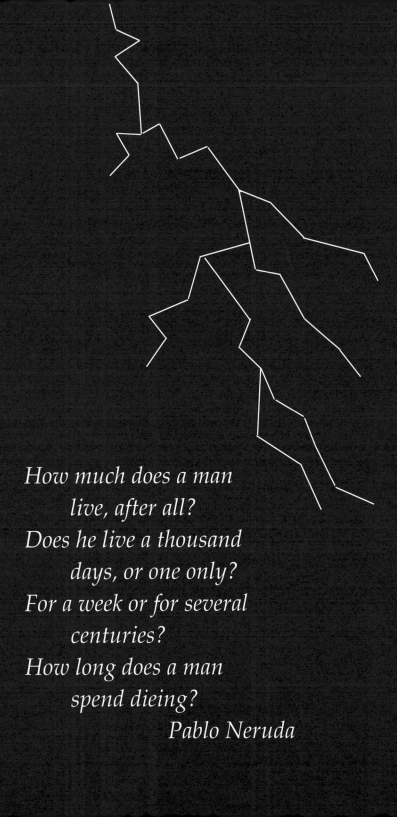

*How much does a man
      live, after all?
Does he live a thousand
      days, or one only?
For a week or for several
      centuries?
How long does a man
      spend dieing?*
                Pablo Neruda

THE WINE COUNTRY

HOTEL LA ROSE

VALLEY OF THE MOON SALOON

MADRONA MANOR

MIGLIAVACCA MANSION

HOTEL LA ROSE

DESPITE ITS ROMANTIC NAME AND DELIGHTFUL EDWARDIAN décor, Hotel La Rose has a very rowdy history.

Lobby of Hotel La Rose.

Built in 1907 by the Italian stonemasons who'd constructed the nearby railroad station—the only building in town that survived the 1906 earthquake —the hotel cost $35,000.   In those days, the handsome sum bought forty rooms and a bar—a very lively bar.

Legend has it that during Prohibition, the La Rose never stopped serving red wine despite the fact that one of Santa Rosa's finest narrowly escaped being tarred and feathered for attempting to shut them down.

During this period a family of three checked into the hotel. When the second floor room assigned them proved too small, the parents kept it for themselves and another was found for their small boy on the fourth floor.

At night before the boy went to bed, he came down to say goodnight to his parents. The routine continued for two nights. On the third the parents were sitting in their room when bandits broke in and shot them. When the boy came down for his goodnight kiss, he found his mother and father dead. The bandits had broken into their room by mistake.

Staff members believe the little boy still haunts the stairs and hall hunting for his parents. A doctor who was staying in the hotel woke in the middle of the night to the sound of someone crying. It seemed so urgent that he got up and went looking to see if someone needed him. The doctor walked up and down the halls but could find no source. "Who's crying?" he asked the desk clerk. "Where is it coming from?"

The desk clerk merely shrugged; he heard nothing. The doctor was so distraught that he packed up and checked out.

Valjean Hill, the night auditor, feels she's never alone in the La Rose at night. In her case, the energy is playful rather than tragic. "I feel him—I think it's a him—running up and down the halls. He likes to play, like any kid," she says. "I've never seen him but I know he's there and sometimes I can hear him laugh."

Sobbing? Laughing? The verdict is still out.

The Wine Country

Hotel La Rose, 308 Wilson St., Santa Rosa.   (800) 527-6738.

VALLEY OF THE MOON SALOON

THERE ARE SPIRITS AND THEN THERE ARE SPIRITS, OBVIOUSLY not all are found in bottles. Carolina Ceelen, owner of the Valley of the Moon Saloon, is certain of that.

Carolina Ceelan.
Photograph by A. May.

Ceelan says that she's had numerous close encounters—of the spooky kind—and seen enough apparitions in the two room, 100 year old bar to *know* the place is haunted.

Several customers, the upstairs tenant, and a few employees are equally sure — and they all insist that this isn't the kind of spirit that appears only after a stiff belt or a few beers.

It all began with records that inexplicably popped out of their secured slots in the juke box. Then the sound of pool balls hitting one another was heard when no one was playing—no one human, that is. Money in the cash register which had been carefully counted, sorted and bound with rubber bands was found strewn about the drawer, yet none was missing. Several patrons sat spellbound as they watched bicycles stored in the back room suddenly sway back and forth only to stop abruptly as if someone or some*thing* has grabbed them.

David Wooster, who occupies the apartment above the saloon, was a bit dubious about moving in when the former tenant told him of a bar of soap that just floated into his hand while he showered one morning—as though some obliging soul had handed it to him. But the cheap rent convinced him to take a chance and he hasn't been sorry.

"The ghost isn't a bad roommate," he says. "It's pretty much live and let live—or something like that; but he does have one idiosyncrasy. It's the pantry door. He wants it closed. When I forget, he has a way of letting me know. Suddenly lights go on and off by themselves and things get moved from one room to another."

One afternoon Carolina Ceelen was alone in the pub waiting for the beer distributor, when the ghost touched her arm. Another time it gently patted her posterior.

Valley of the Moon Saloon. Photograph by A. May.

What can one conclude about this ghost that may—or may not—be a carry over from the Indian burial grounds that once comprised the area?

Perhaps this is an easy-going kind of spirit. He appears to enjoy the small town pub atmosphere with its clutter of video games, wooden stools and walls covered with mirrors, posters and neon lights all advertising beer. Apparently he enjoys being where the action is and occasionally can't restrain himself from being a part of it.

Surely one thing is certain: this ghost is still human enough to enjoy the companionship of a very pretty woman.

The Valley of the Moon Saloon is no longer in business. It was located at 17154 Sonoma Highway, Sonoma.

The Wine Country

MADRONA MANOR:
The Ghost & Mrs. Muir

THEY CALL THEM PAINTED LADIES—THOSE FRAGILE OLD Victorians gussied up in bright colors, held together by prayers. It was just such a structure that seemed a dream come true to Carol Muir.

While in Saudi Arabia, Carol and her husband, John Muir, a Bechtel executive, had dreamed of becoming innkeepers. Fantasy took a quantum leap toward reality when the

Madrona Manor

couple put last things first. While vacationing in Nepal, Carol and John visited a rosewood factory where, "on an impulse" they placed an order for ten tables, forty chairs, ten mirror frames, trim for forty doors and one magnificent front door. Now they *had* to do it!

Returning to California, they proceeded to search for the "perfect house." Cruelly, it eluded them. No place was right until one day Carol came to the slumbering town of Healdsburg where, quite by chance, she peeked through a locked iron gate catching a glimpse of John Paxton's mansion.

Healdsburg has always been a place where days move quietly. In Paxton's time it was known as the buckle of Sonoma's prosperous prune-belt.

Today the town is surrounded by three internationally known vineyards, yet appears strangely unaware of its new found popularity. The unpretentious charm of this "in" spot is like the modesty of a young duckling suddenly discovering itself a swan.

Surveying a Gothic Victorian mansion with its wraparound veranda and mansard roof, Carol wondered about the former occupants. Who had walked within those walls, loving, laughing, crying? What angry words were spoken there? As she spoke with oldtimers and searched Sonoma County records, a family saga emerged. The property was acquired in 1879 by John Alexander Paxton, a state legislator who having made a fortune in mining, banking, lumber, was ready to turn his attention to Sonoma's fledgling wine industry.

Townspeople were awed by the entrepreneur and watched fascinated as his grand mansion, set on a knoll surrounded by towering trees took form. In 1880 the showplace was complete and a year later Paxton purchased the 40 acre Sterling Ranch where he established a thriving winery. Then, in 1887, Hannah Paxton received word that her husband had died of a sudden heart attack on a steamer while returning from a business trip to Liverpool. The body was returned to Hannah who is said to have kept it in a leadlined, glass coffin *in the house* until her own death in 1902.

The couple's two sons, Blitz and Charles, inherited the dynasty. Blitz, who took over the family home as well as the presidency of the Bank of Santa Rosa, shocked the community by deserting his wife and their two children to marry another woman. Charles took his life after his wife deserted him for another man. The

The Wine Country

Paxton mansion was sold in 1913 and passed from one owner to another until it at last stood empty and waiting.

Carol Muir's first inkling that the house just might be haunted came early in 1982 shortly after she and her husband had purchased it. A crew of carpenters from Red Bluff would drive down late Sunday, working and camping in the house until their return home on Friday. "None of them saw anything, but all spoke of feeling a *presence*," she recalls. "Later some of the staff felt a sense of being watched and guests complained of things being moved to strange, unexpected places. I thought it was nonsense."

That was before Carolyn Yarbrough and her article in the *Los Angeles Times*. "There isn't much to do in Healdsburg or Madrona Manor after dinner," Yarbrough wrote in an account published in 1985. "Night falls like a great black curtain over the entire estate. Guests dawdle as long as possible over dinner and after dinner liqueurs."

But, as Yarbrough went on to describe to her readers, there would be a thrill she hadn't bargained for before the night was through.

But Yarbrough was to have a thrill she hadn't bargained for before the night was over. Retiring to room 101 she fell asleep almost immediately, but awakened suddenly to confront a woman, possibly in her mid- 30s, wearing a long black dress, a narrow black ribbon fastening her white Peter Pan collar.

"I closed my eyes," the reporter wrote, "forcing myself to breathe more slowly. When I felt more in control, I opened my eyes with fearful trepidation. The woman had moved and was sitting in the blue velvet chair by the window. 'What do you want?' I asked. There was no answer and as I watched, straining to make out more details, the slender form dissolved."

The phenomenon was the topic of much speculation at breakfast the next morning. Though many scoffed, a waitress appeared merely surprised.

"Actually," she pointed out, "you weren't even in the haunted room.

Rooom 101, Madrona Manor

It's 201 where all the strange things have been happening."

On June 19, 1986 Bill and San Dee Partirdge of Buena Park, California, were guests at the Madrona Manor. Upon completing their dinner, SanDee was startled to see one of the French doors open and a small gray haired lady dressed in the clothing of the last century enter the room. No one else was aware of her, but as SanDee continued to stare, the woman approached. "I'm glad that you can see me," she said. "I feel so badly sometimes that no one can. This was my house once and I like what's been done to it. I'd like to tell someone that—now you can tell them."

At first SanDee couldn't bring herself to discuss what had happened. Her husband had been sitting beside her the entire time and had seen nothing; but when she returned home, SanDee felt compelled to write to Carol Muir confiding her experience.

And as for Mrs. Muir, what does she think about her ghost? "Well, things do happen," she admitted to me. "Once at breakfast a woman literally shrieked because a coffee cup revolved on its saucer right before her eyes. It's hard to ignore *that* kind of

The Wine Country

evidence. Recently guests from Santa Barbara, Dean Mars, a well known sculptor, and his wife, Melinda, presented me with crystal chips accompanied by elaborate instructions for placing them in holes marking the four corners of the property. These 'sentinels" would guard and protect me, they explained. I followed the advice — it could hardly do any harm."

Madrona Manor

Attractive, gregarious, highly efficient, this Mrs. Muir, unlike her fey movie namesake, would rather brag about her son's cooking—Todd, a graduate of the California Culinary Academy, worked at the famed Chez Panisse Restaurant before coming to the Madrona—or discuss the inn's extensive prize winning wine list, than ponder ghostly possibilities.

"If you can say live and let live about a ghost, that's how I feel," she explains. "I don't bother them—they don't bother me. We're all happy."

The Madrona Manor is located at 1001 Westside Road, Healdsburg, 95448. Phone: (707)433-4231

MIGLIAVACCA MANSION

PERHAPS ONLY AN INMATE ON DEATH ROW AWAITING A LAST minute reprieve could fully appreciate the tale of the Migliavacca Mansion.

The Migliavacca Mansion. Photograph by Vern Applyby.

The Wine Country

Condemned to demolition, facing certain destruction again and again, the historic landmark in downtown Napa has clung tenuously to life, one last minute stay of execution after another, delaying the inevitable.

Many fine Victorians have endured similar cliffhangers in recent years only to quietly give up the ghost. But the Magiliavacca house is not just another Victorian. Not only is it an integral part of Napa Valley's living legend, but it possesses a spirit that stubbornly refuses to vacate the premises—despite the fact that the building itself has been moved twice.

The story has its beginnings in 1833 with the birth of Giacomo Migliavacca in Italy. Migrating to the United States as a boy, he settled in Napa, opening a small grocery store in 1867. Soon the store was known for its fine wine selection and before long Migliavacca was creating his own varieties. What began as a bathtub venture grew and prospered, and in 1880 land was purchased and a winery constructed. Giacomo, his wife, Marie, and their children — eventually numbering thirteen — lived upstairs.

In 1895 work began on their impressive Queen Anne mansion, a lighter, airier design which developed as an alternative to the starker, more Gothic lines of the classic English Victorian. Constructed of the finest materials available, the house reflected essential Queen Anne elements—rounded tower, steep gabled roof and varied textures—at their loveliest. The upper two stories were imported Italian slate shingles over redwood sheeting and the prominent corner turret had a slate roof and curved windows. Stained glass windows were another prominent feature. The first floor consisted of a front parlor, sitting room and reception hall complete with a "coachman's corner," where visitor's coachmen awaited their employers. An oak staircase led to the second floor with its center hallway, five bedrooms and full Victorian bath. The third floor was designed as a grand ballroom. All trim was handcarved redwood, with the exception of the handcarved oak reception area. The details and quality of materials make modern architectural duplication virtually impossible.

After Giacomo Migliavacca's death, his son James, became a director of the Bank of Italy, later the Bank of America. Another son, Laurence, took over the family winery. With the death of the Angelina in 1921, last member of the immediate family, the once proud mansion sank into a genteel decline standing empty until finally sold by the family in 1925.

During World War II, the second and third floors were divided into small sleeping rooms to house Mare Island employees. Among them was Anna Wurz and her family who complained often to Jess Doud, now executive director of the Napa County Historical Society, that the house was haunted. Night after night the Wurz family, occupying the top floor—formerly the ballroom—was awakened by the sound of footsteps approaching them on the stairs. Opening the door, they were confronted by darkness. There were other sounds too: laughter and old fashioned music. The Wurz family wanted nothing more than to leave, but housing was in short supply during the war.

When the world conflict ended, the house stood empty. There were other owners but no one ever remained for long. Then in 1970, the property was purchased by Napa County for $20,400 and demolition was scheduled to make way for a new library. At the last minute, Trost Housemovers came to the rescue. The house was jacked up and moved one block to the bank of the Napa River, awaiting a barge trip to a new location in Benicia.

Bureaucratic roadblocks shattered that hope. Benicia didn't want a "potential fire trap—least of all one with a ghost." Another potential buyer surfaced with plans to relocate the house a short distance down river. More redtape strangled that idea.

Meanwhile the Migliavacca house in its isolated riverside location

The Wine Country

was an easy mark for vandals and looters who used chain saws to remove the staircase and light fixtures. Many preservationists questioned whether a professional demolition job wasn't preferable to a slow, torturous death. Jackals of the night were literally tearing the house to pieces.

Migliavacca Mansion side entrance.

Condemned once more, a last minute reprieve was sought by Tom Connell. Young, inexperienced, idealistic—Connell resolved to do the job that had totally defied the so-called experts. In 1975, he moved the Magliavacca house for a second time, selecting a lot close to its original location. Full of confidence, he predicted that the mansion would be fully restored within six months. In reality, the project took three years. Often work ground to a total stop, the building standing forlornly, smothered by scaffolding, interior gutted.

But Connell's perseverance paid off. Today the Magiliavacca Mansion is again a showplace and has been listed on the National Register of Historic Places. Once more the building radiates Victorian splendor — though the top floor is no longer used as a ballroom, nor do coachmen wait in the front hallway. Divided into seven offices, the mansion now houses myriad interests. Laughter is anything but eerie, cheerful voices echo through the halls, brisk footsteps are heard.

But at night. . . .well no one ever really likes to work too late.........

The Migliavacca Mansion is located at 1475 Fourth Street, Napa.

The Wine Country

I do not feel myself authorized to reject all ghost stories; for however improbable one taken alone might appear, the mass of them taken together command credence.
                    —Immanuel Kant

NORTHERN COAST

EASKOOT HOUSE

THE HAUNTED DOLL HOUSE

MILL COTTAGE—
JENNER INN & COTTAGES

MENDOCINO INN

EASKOOT HOUSE

SURELY THE MOST GHOSTLY GHOST AROUND IS CAPTAIN ALFRED Easkoot, who wanders the misty shores of Marin on stormy nights searching, searching searching for his golden hook.

In life, Easkoot had a withered hand to which a golden hook was fixed. In death, as his casket was carried across the sand, the hook somehow became detached and was washed out to sea.

It would be hard to find a more classic example of folk fantasy and yet there are many over the years who claim to have seen the shadowy form of the old sea captain silhouetted against the dunes of Stinson Beach. Still more have testified to poltergeist phenomena in the captain's house.

Alfred Derby Easkoot was born in Manchester, Massachusetts, on February 3, 1820. At the age of nine, he went to sea as a cabin boy. Fours years later he was severely injured in a fire at sea that scarred his face and turned one hand into a withered claw.

After his recovery, young Easkoot went back to sea, eventually becoming a ship's captain and master of a merchant ship sailing between Philadelphia and South America. Later Captain Easkoot's own lumber schooner went aground on Duxbury Reef near Stinson Beach. He survived the wreck and built a house from the remnants that washed ashore, then went on to become Marin County's first surveyor and a successful business man.

He lived alone and apparently content until he fell in love with Amelia Dumas, a wealthy and stylish Philadelphian. How the crusty old salt managed to woo and wed a beautiful and elegant woman with the romantic name of of Amelia is another mystery, but he did.

The captain's snug cabin was torn down and redesigned to suit the taste of his eastern bride. The original timbers may still be seen in the stairway of the graceful New England Colonial.

Easkoot made wise land invest- ments and ten years after his wedding in 1871, retired from surveying and es- tablished a resort-campground called Easkoot's Beach, where the public beach is today.

Easkoot house as it is today. Photograph by Vern Appleby.

The captain was a beloved figure among vacation- ers at the beach. He took visitors on fishing trips, played with children and presided over sing-a-longs and taffy pulls.

Life went well for Easkoot until 1886 when Amelia rose from the dinner table in great pain and collapsed. She died in Easkoot's arms. There were rumors of foul play by the captain, but an autopsy revealed that she'd died of a ruptured heart.

Easkoot was alone again but no longer contented with his lot. The once outgoing businessman became an embittered recluse who patrolled the beach with a spyglass searching for trespassers. The proud manor house was allowed to fall into disrepair until it was almost obscured by vines and bushes. It's said that it was at this time that the captain affixed a golden hook to his withered hand.

Northern Coast

Competition developed between Easkoot and Nathan Stinson—the Point Reyes dairy farmer for whom the town was named—for the area's seashore business. The rivalry became an obsession that absorbed Easkoot until his death of a heart attack on December 10, 1905.

That Easkoot's home would eventually become the property of a Stinson—Eve Stinson Fitzhenry—seems the final irony.

The house enjoyed a brief renaissance during Mrs. Fitzhenry's ownership in the 1930s. Charming gardens were planted and groves of trees—now grown tall, totally concealing the house and blocking the sea view as well. It was during this period that stories began to circulate concerning the place. Doors opened and closed at their own volition. Lights flashed on and off of their own accord. There were unexplainable cold spots and smells. Tales were told of the shadowy figure of a man with a loose, dangling sleeve and a seaman's cap.

It was feared that the captain's soul was tormented, doomed to search forever for his hook. Residents said that every night at 2, the hour of his death, Captain Easkoot came stomping into his home.

A couple who occupied the house were awakened one night by their bed's fierce shaking. Horrified, they saw a shadowy figure leering at them from the foot of the bed—a whiskered gentleman with a seaman's cap and a dangling sleeve. The phantom waved the sleeve, gurgled incoherently, and walked away on creaking shoes.

Soon after, they heard heavy footsteps on the walnut staircase followed by violent thumps against the hollow walls of the attic.

Not surprisingly the house was sold and resold, changing hands several times.

Then in March of 1976 great clouds of smoke were seen pouring from the house. The blaze gutted parts of the interior, blackened

The Easkoot House immediately after the fire.. Photograph by C.J. Marrow.

the outside and destroyed thousands of dollars worth of antiques and paintings. Fortunately no one was in the house at the time. Rumors are rampant but the official fire report, accepted by the insurance company, lists the cause as a defective electric heater. Though many belongings remained about the charred house, the tenants never returned. Their whereabouts are still unknown.

In 1984, Leonard Chapman, personnel manager with the Southern Pacific Transportation Co., and his wife, Judy , dean of students at Dominican College, and their daughter Renata, then, 14, bought the house.

"I know the place has a reputation for being haunted," Chapman told Kevin Leary, a reporter for the *San Francisco Chronicle*, "but I've never seen the ghost. If we have one, I'm sure he's a happy ghost and I'd like to meet him."

"Oh, a few things have happened since we moved in, but they're all explainable — just about."

Northern Coast

Maybe so, but Cinno, the family's 100-pound malamute, apparently doesn't agree. When brought into the house, the hackles of the usually mild mannered dog went up. She dug in her paws and tried to jump out the window, leaving claw marks on the sill. Cinno, a former house dog, now prefers to sleep outside.

A few days after the family moved in, and before their new burglar alarm was hooked up, the alarm bell began ringing for no apparent reason.

"We have an expensive and sophisticated system—it had not been connected and yet there it was ringing at 2 a. m.," Chapman recalls.

He ran up to the attic and tried to disconnect the wires, but the alarm just kept ringing. "I was hugging the bell trying to smother the sound so it wouldn't wake the neighbors; but nothing helped. Then it just shut off by itself after about ten minutes."

Then the action seemed to focus on Renata. She was doing her homework in her bedroom when a scratching noise suddenly began to emanate from under the bed. Renata peered beneath the spread but saw nothing. Then unaccountably the mattress began bouncing up and down.

And so the legend continues. It's easy to imagine that the misanthropic captain continues to view trespassers with hostility. At night when fog shrouds the coast and whitecaps dot the swirling surf, lights may flicker unaccountably inside the house. "Maybe it's the captain," someone invariably suggests.

And who is to say he's wrong?

The Easkoot house, a private home, is located at 3548 Shoreline Highway in Stinson Beach.

THE HAUNTED DOLL HOUSE

WHEN CHARLENE WEBER PURCHASED A CENTURY-OLD HOUSE in Bodega, a parting remark from the former owners was the wish that she liked ghosts.

In 1974 ghosts were the last thing Weber had on her mind. She was busy with plans to open an antique shop and doll museum. If she thought of anything weird it was the town of Bodega itself with its memories of Alfred Hitchcock's thriller *The Birds*. Everywhere Weber looked she was reminded of a horrifying scene from the movie filmed there.

Charlene's Country Treasures... Photograph by A. May.

Fortunately the local birds behaved themselves and Weber began to acquire and display her dolls. These ranged from one half inch to human size. The most bizarre is a life-size effigy of an eight year old girl. As the child lay in her coffin a death mask was made of her face. From this an exact likeness was created and applied to the head of a doll. Before burial, the little girl's long blond hair, eyelashes and eyebrows were removed and attached to the doll's head.

The doll survived the child's grieving parents and on their death joined Charlene Weber's amazing collection. One night not long after she acquired the doll, Weber was awakened by the sound of a zither playing and then a loud crashing noise. Following the eerie music to the second floor, she found the floor littered with broken glass from the case that had housed the effigy doll.

Northern Coast

As she surveyed the doll, Weber realized to her horror that the perpetually smiling expression had given way to one of incredible sadness. Even more amazing was a tiny drop of moisture below one blue eye. Could it have been a tear?

Returning the next morning with a friend, Weber discovered that the doll was not in its usual place. Instead of resting on its customary pedestal, it now stood in the middle of the room. The sad expression of the previous night was gone. Once again the face was lifeless—except for the eyes. The eyes were focused on Weber following her every movement.

Though Charlene Weber has never seen a ghost herself, her guests and customers have. Again and again a visitor will describe a tall man wearing Victorian clothes who bears a striking resemblance to Abraham Lincoln. Some describe the same man dressed in what appears to be a naval uniform. Often he's glimpsed bending over what looks like a child's bed.

Invited to conduct a seance in the house, medium Sylvia Browne made contact with a spirit who identified himself as a sea captain. His name was McCuen, he told her. The spirit spoke of a sick child and appeared to resent the intrusion of strangers in his home.

Later Weber did some research and discovered that a McCuen family had indeed lived in the house nearly one hundred years ago. Even more revealing, there had been a brain damaged child confined to a crib.

At least one guest feels that the old captain takes his proprietorship of the house a bit too far. She was using the bathroom in the museum when the door opened and an apparition of a Lincolnesque man confronted her. She screamed and the man vanished.

Who knows, perhaps the spirit was embarrassed too.

The deserted house that was once Charlene's Country Treasures is located on Bodega Road just past the Salmon Creek Bridge.

MILL COTTAGE— JENNER INN & COTTAGES

ONE AFTERNOON LATE IN SEPTEMBER OF 2005 RACHEL DELOACH was arranging flowers in the hundred year old Mill Cottage—an annex to Jenner Inn. The two-story bungalow is redwood paneled with large windows facing both

Exterior photos of Mill Cottage.

river and sea. Its fabulous and funky—marvelous antiques and stained glass mixed with faded carpets and frayed pillows. Mostly it's old, creaky, squeaky, musty, some say scary.

DeLoach, Jenner Inn's new manager, had heard tales. Some said Mill Cottage is haunted. She didn't believe that.

And then the heavy front door opposite her swung open . . . very slowly. DeLoach stood frozen waiting for someone to come in. No one did. She was alone in the cottage. It must be the wind, she thought. But it wasn't.

That's only one door story. There are so many connected to Mill Cottage. When I stayed there, that same front door seemingly bolted itself from within. A heavy deadbolt. No one was inside.

Northern Coast

Interior photo of Mill Cottage.

That ghosts would manifest themselves at Mill Cottage hardly seems surprising. This magic place where the Russian River joins the sea is a kind of power spot. The meandering river has nourished countless vineyards before reaching its rendezvous with the Pacific. Mill Cottage shares a stunning stretch of coast and estuary with osprey, pelicans, river otters and a colony of some 300 harbor seals.

Jenner itself, a tiny cliffside village, sprouted as a mill town one hundred years ago as opportunists flocked to the area lured by its abundant redwoods. (Jenner lumber largely rebuilt San Francisco following the 1906 quake.) Mill Cottage was once the home of the mill manager. Some say he still haunts the place.

Staff and townspeople believe his name to have been Samuel. Perhaps so. Someone or something calling himself Samuel appears proprietary about the place. One couple staying at the cottage reported seeing his signature appear three times on a bathroom mirror. Another guest took a picture of the paneled fireplace and was surprised to later view an unknown man standing before the mantle.

The guest journal at Mill Cottage is jammed with references to spectral visitors. Doors open and slam shut of their own accord. Lights go on and off upstairs when no one's there. Matt Bullagher saw faces in the ceiling. Others witnessed apparitions beside the fireplace. Hearing voices is very common. I've heard them too, strange buzzing voices centered somewhere in the depth of the house. Late at night they cut eerily through the incredible stillness. Perhaps you'll hear them too.

Jenner Inn & Cottages. 10400 Coast Rt. 1, Jenner, CA 95450. Phone: (707) 865-0829.

Northern Coast

MENDOCINO HOTEL

THE FACT THAT IT WAS ONCE KNOWN AS THE "TEMPERANCE HOUSE" hasn't dampened spirits at the Mendocino Hotel. In fact, some ghosts are said to hang out at the bar.

The haunted dining room at the Mendocino Hotel.

One can see why. It's a beautiful bar—antique oak beneath a stained glass dome. The bookkeeper wasn't a bit surprised to look in one evening and see a small group of men lounging there. The only trouble was that no one else saw them.

Things like that happen often at the Mendocino Hotel. Consider the time Mary Thompson, the former hotel manager, looked up to see Jack Bush standing at his front desk station, eyes wide, face stark white. "You look like you'd seen a ghost," she joked.

"I just did," he replied. Bush explained that he'd been adding charges on his computer when the hair went up on the back of his neck. There floating before him was a shimmering lady in a see-through nightie.

Another employee, Dorothy Peer-Green, had a more grounded experience. "My ghost wasn't ghostly at all," she says. "She looked like anyone—feet where they should be, right on the floor."

Peer-Green had just entered the back office one evening. Glancing casually through a window into the lounge, Peer-Green was startled to see a beautiful young woman elegantly dressed in the Gibson Girl style. "She was wearing a long green skirt and a white high necked blouse. I watched her for a moment staring out over the bay and then she just disappeared."

Dorothy Peer-Green at the Mendocino Hotel.

Peer-Green seems to be a center of spirit activity. From time to time she hears voices calling "Dottie"—her childhood nickname unknown to others in the hotel. She turns around expecting to see

Northern Coast

someone but never does. When chamber maids reported making up twin beds in Room 10 and then returning with fresh towels a few moments later to find body-shaped indentations in one of the beds, Peer-Green decided to check it out for herself. She went to bed in Room 10 as an experiment, fell asleep, then awakened in the night to feel a presence in the room—"a sort of heaviness."

The Mendocino Hotel has been around long enough to attract a legion of ghosts. It's the only remaining hotel from a time when Mendocino was a booming port for the logging trade—20,000 people then as opposed to 1000 today. Loggers were a rowdy bunch, it's said. The town was home to nineteen saloons and no shortage of pool halls and "fast houses."

The hotel, then called *The Temperance House* was considered "the bastion of good Christian morals in a town of loggers." The original structure dates from 1878 and encompasses the present lobby, bar, dining room, kitchen and upstairs rooms. The lobby is warmed by a Dutch polished steel fireplace, dated 1799. An old Midwestern bank teller's booth serves as the front desk. The effect is so inviting, it's small wonder that some spirits never want to leave.

Guests, as well as staff, have reported seeing ghosts. One took a tumble on the empty wooden staircase and complained that an unknown presence had pushed him. More pleasantly, dining guests have from time to time reported seeing the apparition of a Victorian lady—gowned in blue—reflected in the mirrors behind tables 6 and 8.

The apparitions aren't confined to the original building. In Room 307—one of the garden annexes—a boy staying with his mother watched with amazement as a mirror clouded and a man's face slowly appeared. He called his mother and the two watched the apparition for a full five minutes before it slowly faded away.

History lies close to the surface in Mendocino. Timbers and brick footings may still be seen on the headlands—remnants of lumber loading chutes. Flowers bloom wild where once carefully-tended flowers used to grow. Rusted chains and iron fittings represent the hopes and determination of early settlers, but more telling are the many widows' walks—the rooftop balconies where wives scanned the sea for the sight of a familiar sail. When the foggy mists roll in Mendocino is a haunted place.

Mendocino Hotel & Garden Suites. 45080 Main St. Mendocino, CA 95460 Phone (707) 937-0511.

The haunted table at the Mendocino Hotel.

Northern Coast

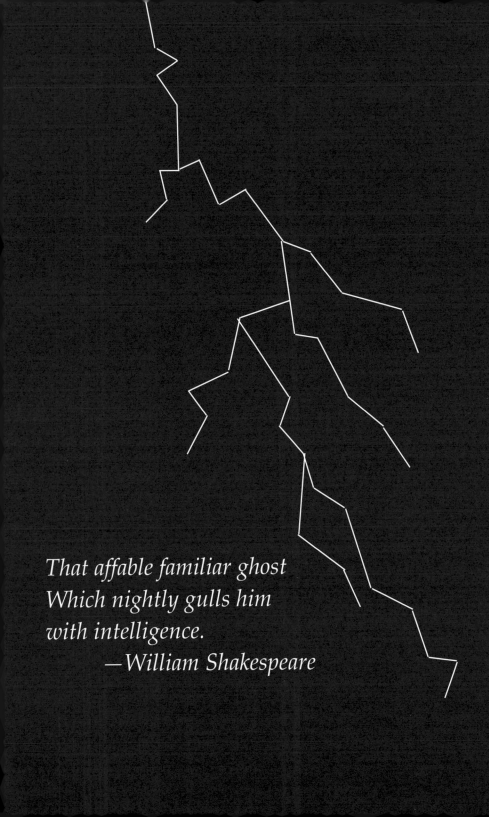

That affable familiar ghost
Which nightly gulls him
with intelligence.
　　—William Shakespeare

MOTHER LODE COUNTRY/THE SIERRA

AHWAHNEE LODGE

WILLOW HOTEL

BATHROOM MACHINERIES

DORRINGTON HOTEL

HOTEL LEGER

SUTTER CREEK INN

VINEYARD HOUSE

NEVADA COUNTY HISTORICAL MUSEUM

LANEY HOUSE

CAL-NEVA RESORT

TRUCKEE HOTEL

AHWAHNEE LODGE

Ahwahnee Lodge in winter. Below, interior view. Photos courtesy of Ahwahnee Lodge.

THAT YOSEMITE'S WORLD FAMOUS LODGE WOULD HAVE
been given a Native American
name is hardly surprising, yet few
are aware that Ahwahnee means
"gaping mouth." The name
merely refers to the Yosemite valley, but still sounds eerie.

The Lodge stands today because
Stephen Mather, first director of
the National Park Service, loved
Yosemite and dreamed of sharing its beauties on a year-round
basis. A world class hotel was
what Mather had in mind when,
in 1925, he commissioned the
Yosemite Park and Curry Company (YP&C Co.) to build one.

In 1927 Donald Tressider, YP&C Co. president, and his wife, Mary, developed the million dollar lodge which they operated for many years. The couple was fascinated by local Native American history. It was Mary who came up with the gaping mouth name and it is she who is said to haunt the lodge.

After her husband's death, Mary Curry Tressider resided in the uppermost floor of the Ahwahnee. Following her demise in 1970, the apartment was converted into guest rooms. It's in this area that staff and guests feel Mary's loving presence and sometimes see her shadowy form.

Yet another ghost haunting the Ahwahnee is thought to be that of former president John F. Kennedy—or at least his rocking chair. Housekeepers report seeing or hearing a moving rocking chair in the third floor parlor—a place that doesn't ordinarily have a rocking chair. Invariably when someone comes to check out the claim, the chair has vanished.

Jack Hicks, the Ahwahnee's long time maitre'd, recalls that a rocking chair was brought in for Kennedy's comfort while he stayed there and removed after the president's departure. Disappointingly, only the apparition of the chair is seen, not the president himself.

The Ahwahnee Lodge, Yosemite National Park. Phone: (559) 252-4848

Ahwahnee Lodge in winter. Photo courtesy of Ahwanhee Lodge.

The Mother Lode Country/The Sierra

WILLOW HOTEL

FIRST IT WAS THE SITE OF A LYNCHING—-A MAN WAS summarily hung.   Later there were at least three violent deaths triggered by the pressures of frontier life.   Finally there was a mine disaster killing twenty-three men.

Small wonder that the Willow Hotel built in 1862 on the site of these tragedies—collapsed mine shaft, lynching and violence resulting in multiple deaths—would have questionable vibes.

But there's even another reason. Psychic researcher and medium, the late Nick Nocerino said that the most likely cause of the chronic fires that have plagued the building — at least five of them in the last decade — was the Jamestown Fire of 1896. In that dreadful holocaust, the town had no water to fight the fire, so locals resorted to dynamite to stifle the flames. Most of the town was devastated—save the Willow Hotel. Nocerino believed that that long ago bad luck has triggered an enduring resentment among the ghosts of people who were killed in the blaze and subsequent explosions.

In an attempt to placate them, the medium conducted an exorcism of the building.   Nine spirits were contacted on October 1978. "I could reason with six of them," he told me, "but there are three others who are still angry. I'm afraid they'll be back and they'll take something else with them."

Sadly enough Nocerino's prediction came true. On July 20, 1985 yet another mystery blaze not only destroyed the hotel annex, but a nearby barbershop, jewelry store and food market.   The fire began with what appeared to have been an overheated refrigerator and then went straight up to the Hanging Room on the second floor, the first room to burn. The "hanging room,"—dark, spooky

The Willow Hotel circa 1862

hardly more than a closet—got its name from the deaths of two men, strangers to one another, who hung themselves there on two consecutive nights.

Many priceless antiques were consumed by flames. The building, thought to be the oldest surviving hotel in the Mother Lode constructed totally of wood, was gutted. Amazingly, the ancient bar constructed of exquisitely joined mahogany, rosewood and redwood burl, where the infamous gun slinger Bat Masterson had once lounged, remained in tact.

During the efforts to reconstruct the building, Mike Cusentino, a bartender, was sleeping upstairs. One night he was awakened in the middle of the night by a man his 60's wearing pajamas and a bathrobe, who angrily stared down at him before disappearing.

Then, late one winter night Kevin Mooney, part owner of the restaurant, was locking up when a glimpse out the back window stopped him cold. "There were these two beet-red eyes staring back at me," he recalled. "I never saw anything like it. Finally I

The Mother Lode Country/The Sierra

got up nerve enough to open the door, but it wouldn't move. Seems like it took hours to get it open. Once I did, there was no one--no *thing* there."

It wasn't the end. Tom Thorton and Steve Hagel, caretakers of the gutted building, spent several fearsome nights as the very walls seemed to take on a frightening will of their own. "There were weird, wild noises—nothing that we could identify, nothing human," they attempted to explain later.

The Willow Hotel after the last fire.

Though the hotel itself was never rebuilt, the building, still known as the Willow Hotel, continues as a restaurant and bar. Patrons and employees alike report seeing "a frizzy redhead," believed to be Elualah Sims who was murdered by her husband in the bar nearly 100 years ago. There's another apparition as well, a small, furtive man who wanders through the halls as though searching for someone.

And yet another ghost frequently appears who looks like a gambler straight from central casting complete with dapper mustache and immaculate black suit. He's more aggressive than the other spirits, appearing at the bar—only to disappear when served. Look around next time you're in the area, perhaps he'll deal you a hand.

The Willow Hotel is located on the corner of Main and Willow streets in Jamestown. Telephone: (209) 984-3998.

BATHROOM MACHINERIES

BATHROOM MACHINERIES HAS SOMETHING GUARANTEED to yank your chain. Not only does the emporium have antique plumbing, lighting, keys and hardware, but a resident ghost. The hundred-year-old I.O.O.F Hall is high spirited to say the least—just ask the folks who work there.

Tom Scheller, the business's owner, had been hearing and seeing things about the place since 1976. Then not long ago two prospective customers he'd not met before came in. The couple started up the stairs to look at tubs on the second floor. Suddenly they stopped in their tracks, paused and turned around. They had felt a presence on the stairs, "saw" a woman's form stumble and hurtle downward. The couple knew that the woman had died as a result of the fall.

"It really didn't surprise me," Scheller said. "Only a week before I'd heard noises on the stairs and run up to investigate. The motion light in an upstairs room went on before I could get there. I was six or eight stairs away, the ghost was just ahead of me. I call it the ghost. What else can it be—there was nothing human or animal up there."

John Vienop, a clerk, was joking with Scheller about the now legendary ghost when a soap dish suddenly flipped off a shelf. "There was no way that it could have slid off by itself."

Another time Vienop and Brian Wynne, another employee, were speculating about the ghost while moving an antique tub. "Just then a tub shelf from another tub flipped up at us. We tried jumping around, thinking that vibrations might have caused it but that was clearly not the cause."

The Mother Lode Country/The Sierra

Jim Muller, another long time employee, has often heard footsteps coming from the floor above when he was alone in the store. "I went up to investigate and a door slammed shut in my face. Other times merchandise has just flown off the shelf. There was no breeze, just a big 'boom!' as it landed on the floor."

Once while working upstairs, he saw a woman out of the corner of his eye. He turned to say, "May I help you?" and she disappeared.

Why should a bathroom supply house be haunted? Nobody knows. The building enjoyed lively days when it housed the I.O.O.F. Hall. Echoes of laughter and conversation are still heard by all three men. It's also known that club members were embalmed in the building and that commemorative bricks are imbedded in the floor. Perhaps, too, the vintage fixtures—tubs and toilets—dating from before the Civil War carry a kind of psychic energy. It's all very human—in an inhuman sort of way.

Bathroom Machineries

Bathroom Machineries is located at 495 Main St., Murphys. (209) 728-2031. Open weekdays, 8 to 5, Saturdays 10 to 4. Closed Sundays.

DORRINGTON HOTEL

IN 1852, WHEN REBECCA DORRINGTON GARDNER WITH HER husband, John, built their small inn as a stagecoach stop, Big Trees Carson Valley toll road was little more than a trail. A rider starting from the nearest town at sunrise on a summer day, might hope to arrive by late evening. Few but herders and stock men cared to make the journey.

Today Highway 4 is a popular route linking the San Joaquin Valley with the high Sierras. Skiers, vacationers and locals flock to the busy hotel with its lively bar and thriving restaurant.

Rebecca Dorrington Gardner's maiden name was adopted by the mountain town that grew up around the Gardner hostelry. According to Bonnie Saville, who with her husband, Arden, bought the inn in 1977, Rebecca has never left.

"I began to feel her presence right away," Bonnie says today. "It wasn't exactly welcoming. Arden and I were the first owners to make changes since the Gardners built the place. Rebecca didn't like that at all. I kept the restaurant open from 6 a.m. till ten at night which meant that my husband couldn't begin his carpentry work until quite late. Rebecca let him work until three, then she'd start acting out. The radio shut itself off, extension cords came unplugged, lights went on and off by themselves."

Over the years Rebecca seems to have come to accept the renovations as well as the Savilles—most of the time. "Rebecca has very definite ideas about what she likes and doesn't like," Bonnie explains. "It would make my life so much easier if she'd just tell me ahead of time that she doesn't want something in her house."

The Mother Lode Country/The Sierra

The Dorrington Hotel

Bonnie cites the time when she bought a stuffed goose to ornament one of the guestrooms. "It was kind of cutesy," she admits, "but I liked it enough to splurge—$75 worth." Bonnie set the goose down on the bed and went off to do her chores about the house. An hour later she returned to find the toy, face down on the floor. This was repeated several times.

Finally Bonnie carried the goose downstairs, muttering to Rebecca all the way. "It isn't enough that I have to explain to my husband how crazy I was to spend $75 on a stuffed goose, now I can't even display it where I want." Bonnie carefully settled the goose on a chair in her office and went to work on her accounts. Several times that morning she had to retrieve the toy from the floor where it had fallen. Or was it pushed? Bonnie, who'd clearly had enough, gave her goose away.

Bonnie's learned the hard way to shop with Rebecca in mind, and, in recent years has been more successful. The incidences of people being locked in their rooms, doors slamming by themselves, curtains moving and strange footsteps have diminished. "I think Rebecca's gotten used to us," Bonnie speculates. "She's clearly drawn to the hotel energy and enjoys the party atmosphere."

Guests often report a shadowy figure who parts the curtains to look out of otherwise unoccupied rooms. A variety of wild stories have been told in an attempt to explain Rebecca's presence in the house. Some claim that Rebecca went out on a cold winter night during a snow storm, lost her way and froze to death. Others say she was massacred by Indians or fell down the hotel stairs and bled to death. The truth is that Rebecca, who outlived her husband, was residing in Altaville when she died of natural causes at 83.

Bonnie, who says she's seen Rebecca several times, believes that the spirit is drawn to the hotel because of her happy life when living there. "The 'ghost' I see isn't an old woman," Bonnie explains. "She's in her early forties, attractive and vibrant." Bonnie frequently smells a fragrance—wild azaleas—that she associates with Rebecca. Sometimes she senses a man's presence—probably John's—and smells Ben Gay. Other times she feels teenage energy that she associates with the Gardners granddaughter, Reba, for whom Mt. Reba was named.

Still, the main presence is Rebecca. "She's always there," Bonnie says, "a part of the house and of our lives. It'll always be her hotel. We're just the caretakers."

Dorrington Hotel, 3431 Highway 4, Dorrington. (209) 795-5800.

The Mother Lode Country/The Sierra

HOTEL LEGER

JERRY WARD'S A CAUTIOUS MAN. FEELING THE EFFECTS OF A LIVELY party at Mokelumne Hill's Hotel Leger, he took a room for the night rather than drive the treacherous Jesus Maria Road to his home some twenty miles away.

Some say George Leger's spirit never checked out of his historic hotel in Mokelumne Hill.

Ward's sound sleep ended abruptly. He wakened suddenly smelling the acrid odor of burnt wood. Switching on a the light, Ward found the room charred almost beyond recognition. A woman knelt in the corner, keening miserably and cradling a baby in her arms.

As he watched frozen with fear, the image slowly faded. The woman disappeared and the room resumed its normal appearance.

"Well, that surely sobered me up!" Ward says today. "I knew I'd never get back to sleep so I got up, dressed and drove home."

That's one story. The hotel has many. One of the most historic hostelries in the Mother Lode, the Leger (pronounced "luh zhay") has always been the center of activity. Beginning in 1851, a hotel has existed on the corner of Lafayette and Main. Until 1866, the building included the county courthouse with a convenient downstairs dungeon and a hanging tree out back.

Since "the Hill" was the biggest, bad-dest, most important mining camp in Calaveras County (according to the records, 17 people killed there in 17 weeks, then five more shot the follow-ing weekend), it scarcely seems surpris-ing that such riotous history would in-spire a legion of restless spirits.

At least that's one theory.

Very little is known for certain. George Leger, born in Germany, but claiming French descent, came to Mokelumne Hill in 1851. Catering to the town's large French population, already ensconced on Lafayette Street, he erected his "inn"—probably a tent—fronting on Main Street.

George Leger

A fire destroyed the hotel in 1854—could Ward have relived the grim aftermath?--but left the stone courthouse still in tact. Within a year the forty-year- old bon vivant was not only back in business but had acquired a wife, Louisa Wilkin, age 23. The 1860 census lists the couple with two children. Ten years later there's no men-tion of Mrs. Leger but there are three children, the youngest named Louisa.

The story goes the mother died in childbirth. Does that explain the eerie sounds of a woman crying that hotel guests report?

People love to embellish the story by saying that Leger was gunned down by an irate husband. It didn't happen. Whatever his indiscretions, the man died of natural causes in 1879. His re-mains were taken from the hotel and interred in a nearby grave-yard. Some say that was the end of it. Some say not.

"George walks the town," insists Ron Miller, the Leger's former owner. "I've seen him. He looks exactly like his picture on the stairs."

The Mother Lode Country/The Sierra

Miller's wife, Joyce, remembers the time she showed a prospective guest through the hotel. Suddenly the woman turned pale and ran outside, later explaining that a spectral man had stood behind Joyce, nodding his head approvingly as she recounted the building's history.

Shortly afterwards the Millers' son, Ronnie, asked them who was staying in "George's room."

"No one right now," his mother replied.

"Oh, yes there is," the boy answered. "A man just came out and asked me to be quiet."

Stories proliferate. In Room 2, guests report seeing a Victorian woman. In Room 3, they see a little boy. Maids make the beds in Rooms 10 and 11, returning later to find them torn up. The wildest story is the midnight cattle drive down Main Street—sounds of mooing, hoof beats and cowbells. Guests—as well as Ashley Canty, a current owner—have rushed to the window only to see a dark, deserted street.

 Ashley's mother, Jane Canty, cleaned the dining room after a party, using three keys to lock three doors before leaving late at night. She returned the next morning, unlocked all the doors and found the room in disarray. Tables were shoved together. Dishes, glasses and silver used. "A hoax seems unlikely," she says. "It was so elaborate—a lot of trouble to execute and difficult to conceal."

Then there's the afternoon that the former hotel manager Shana Molotch leaned against the ice machine in the former dungeon chatting with a plumber. "Is this place haunted?" he asked.

Molotch shrugged. "People believe what they want to believe."

The next moment Molotch became an instant believer when something shoved hard enough to knock her forward. Red marks remained on her shoulder for two days.

Most recently, Molotch was startled when a guest reported seeing a variety of ghosts—three mischievous boys and a man with a mustache who looks like George Leger's photograph. Most specifically, an apparition in Room 11 had a message for her. "Tell Shana that I'm watching."

The guest, who wishes to maintain her privacy, is very clear about what she saw and heard: a spirit with swept up hair and rather drab Victorian clothing who gave her name as Kathleen. Kathleen, she says, is "a strong presence."

Molotch wonders what exactly does the spirit mean? "Is she reassuring me or saying, 'Watch out'?"

The hotel owners decided to call in a team of "ghost busters." Mark Boccuzzi heads Bay Area Paranormal Investigators, assisted by Scott Mossbaugh, co-founder, and five field technicians, Nancy Benson, Stacey Ellis, Ryan Morris and Lori and Jamie Fike. Their "day jobs" include teaching, engineering and accounting.

The wine cellar of the Hotel Leger is a former dungeon.

The team began its case study by drawing a detailed floor plan to establish a frame of reference. Experiments were recorded on the map, tests for environmental anomalies—anything out of the norm.

"Cold hard science is where it's at for us," Boccuzzi says. "We get a visceral rush from exploring something new, finding ways to best examine the situation to determine what's really going on."

The team uses a tri field meter to measure electric magnetic frequencies. They have thermometers to record cold spots, compasses to mark deviations from the field map and a wide variety of cameras and recorders—thousands of dollars worth of highly advanced equipment.

Dagmar Morrow, a Mountain View medium, accompanied the team. At first she felt overwhelmed by impressions. "So many spirits have memories of the hotel," she said. "Imagine 150 years of passion and intrigue. Some of them are rather mischievous. It's as though they're teasing, 'Find out about us if you can'."

Slowly, Morrow sorted them out. In the dungeon, desperate men speculated on their fate. In the lobby George appeared, still keeping tabs on the hotel.

Morrow's most vivid image was the "Gray Lady," a thirtyish woman wearing Victorian clothing—nipped in waist, lace at the cuffs and neckline, a short frilly apron. "She was shy, diffident, looked at me questioningly as if asking, 'Is everything all right?' Some of the young women investigators were drawing diagrams of the hotel. She didn't approve of them sitting on the floor, didn't think it ladylike."

While Morrow communed with her Gray Lady, Boccuzzi detected an electromagnetic anomaly; a column of energy recorded on his tri field meter. When he tested the spot later, the anomaly was gone.

The paranormal investigator is cautious. "Other things can cause this type of disturbance, so I'm hesitant to say that what I detected was directly related to what Dagmar was picking up, but I did find the timing very interesting."

Boccuzzi and his team were up until five, prowling every room with their video cameras and recorders. Their data proved inconclusive, but no one's giving up. "We hope to return soon to the Leger to resume our investigations," Boccuzzi says. "What better use is there for our spare time than the attempt to document the survival of the human spirit?"

The Hotel Leger is located at 8304 Main, Mokelumne Hill. (209) 286-1401.

SUTTER CREEK INN

THE SUTTER CREEK INN IS ALIVE WITH GHOSTS—BOTH NICE and naughty.

The Sutter Creek Inn. Photograph by C.J. Marrow.

Not only does the house—a New England clapboard—attract phenomena, so does its owner, Jane Way.

Jane bought the house in 1966. "Just why, I can't imagine," she says today. "It was an all time low in my life. My son had been killed in an accident.   My husband and I had just split. My health was terrible—I'd had cancer twice. I was feeling very, very sorry for myself."

Soon after, while passing through San Francisco, she stopped on an impulse at a spiritualist church. "It was a crazy thing to do," she admits. "I was just driving down a street looking for an on-ramp to the freeway and saw the sign. I'd never been there before, never had known anyone who had—but suddenly there I was parking my car and walking in."

"The minister was Florence Becker, a very gifted medium. We'd never met before. Of course she couldn't have known a thing about me—and yet she seemed to know everything. 'You've just lost your son,' she said almost immediately and then began to describe him in detail. Her description was so accurate that I began to cry.'

"'You've bought an old place in the mountains,' she continued. 'I see people coming and going—it must be a hotel. That's right for you—but you must stop the bitterness. It could ruin everything. Keep on with what you're doing but without bitterness. You'll be successful.'"

Jane Way left the church and drove back to Sutter Creek. Again and again her mind returned to the medium's words. Then a few nights later she saw her first ghost.

"It was Saturday evening and all the hotel guests were out," she recalls. "I was getting ready to leave also; some friends were having a costume party. Suddenly conscious of being watched, I looked up. There was a tall man wearing old fashioned looking clothes standing in the doorway. For a moment I thought he must be going to the same party. I heard the words: *I will protect your inn*. He smiled and then faded away.

"Well, really, how could I be bitter after an experience like that? Surely somebody out of this world had decided to take an interest in my affairs. What more could anyone ask? I suppose what had bothered me most was the apparent futility of life, its seeming transience. Now here in my own house was living proof of the continuity of the human spirit."

Way believes that this was the spirit of State Senator Edward Convers Voorhies who had lived in the house for many years.

The house had originally been built in 1860 by John Keyes as a home for his young bride, Clara McIntire. It was hoped its New

England lines would ease the loneliness for her native New Hampshire. The couple had one child who died of diphtheria when still a baby. Then in 1875 Keyes died leaving Clara a widow at thirty-four.

Two years later Voorhies came to town and proceeded to court her. They were married on March 29, 1880. The couple had two children. Earl died in infancy, but Gertrude lived to be ninety.

"I bought the house from Gertrude just before she moved to a rest home," Way explains. "She'd lived in the place all her life and was very attached to it. I suppose that's why her spirit returned one evening as several guests were gathered in the living room—she just wanted to check on things."

Way's experience with Senator Voorhies, following so soon after the psychic reading, seems to have triggered a mediumship within herself. In the intervening years she experienced a wide variety of psychic phenomena.

There was a German ophthalmologist who tried to help me with an eye problem. He didn't—but I know his intentions were good," she says.

Way's less certain about a spectral exhibitionist—a flasher. "He seemed very proud of his endowments," she recalls. "I think he'd been punished in some way in his earthly life, possibly been mutilated. You'd think death would be the end of earthly hang-ups; but, if he's any indication, we take them with us.

"Once a cat was flung against the wall by an unseen force—possibly a ghost who doesn't like cats. They don't like garlic either, I've discovered. If you don't want ghosts, a good fettuccine should eliminate any chance of an encounter."

A very good remedy to keep in mind.

The Sutter Creek Inn is located at 75 Main Street, Sutter Creek. Telephone: (209) 267-5606.

The Mother Lode Country/The Sierra

VINEYARD HOUSE

LOUISE ALLHOFF MUST HAVE BEEN A HARD WOMAN TO LIVE WITH.

There was a first husband, a successful vintner, who committed suicide in a Virginia City outhouse.

Then along came Robert Chalmers, the merchant prince of the Gold Rush capital, Coloma.   Attracted to the beautiful widow with her easy elegance and proud, imperious ways, Chalmers persuaded her to marry him.   For a time they were a formidable team.   Chalmers had the hustle, Louise had the class.   They enlarged her vineyards and won prizes for their wines.   Chalmers was elected to the State legislature. While his financial empire continued to grow, she introduced "culture" to the area.

At the apex of their success, this pair of high rollers constructed a

four-story man-sion which was to be a mecca for the Mother Lode elite. Among the attractions of their "Vineyard House" was a ninety-foot ball-room and a music room.

The Vineyard House. Photograph by C. J. Marrow.

But Robert Chalmers' pleasure was brief. Soon after completion of the showplace in 1878, his manner began to change.   The former orator now spoke in whispers.   Seeing a grave being dug in the cemetery across the street, he walked over and laid down to see if it would fit him.

Soon—according to Louise — Chalmers was a raving maniac and she was forced to chain him in the cellar of their home. It was said that she came down often to taunt him, standing always just beyond his frenzied grasp. Chalmers' misery lasted for nearly three years. In 1881, he starved to death, fearing that Louise was trying to poison him.

The bar in the cellar jail.
Photograph by C.J.Marrow.

Call it divine retribution or merely bad luck, hard times befell Louise. A blight attacked her grapes. The Chinese immigrants who slept in the vineyard to keep deer out were expelled in a pogrom and the remaining grapes ravaged by humans and animals. Their real estate holdings had dwindled during Chalmers' illness and the bank foreclosed on the Vineyard House.

Louise was allowed to remain on a rent paying basis; but, in order to do so, was forced to take in roomers and to allow the cellar to be used as an auxiliary jail. At least two prisoners spent their last night on earth there. One was a school teacher who had killed a student, the other a highway- man. The teacher recited poetry from the scaffold, the highwayman danced a jig and then burst into tears.

Louise died, lonely and impoverished, in 1913. The proud mansion where Ulysses S. Grant once made a speech fell into melancholy decay as a series of owners came and went, always complaining of unaccountable sounds. One tenant left suddenly in the middle of the night, refusing to talk about what he'd seen.

In 1956 the house was turned into an inn and restaurant. Drinks are now served in the cellar jail where thieves, murderers and Robert Chalmers once languished. Dave Vanbuskirk, one of the

The Mother Lode Country/The Sierra

owners, often heard unexplained steps on the stairs and seen a doorknob turn before his startled eyes — with no one on the other side. Once in the seemingly empty house a freshly made bed came unmade and the impression of a form could clearly be seen on the sheets. The fact that Vanbuskirk had, himself, found a stack of old coffins under the front porch shortly after buying the place did little to cheer him.

During the night guests reported hearing the sound of chains rattling, rustling skirts, heavy breathing and brisk steps. One San Francisco couple heard a raucous group enter by the front door and climb the stairs laughing loudly. Going to the door to quiet the revelers, they saw three men dressed in Victorian clothing fade before their eyes.

Darlene and Frank Herrera, who purchased the house in 1974, tried to play down the "ghost stuff." They worked hard to make the place genuinely Victorian with a variety of museum quality antiques.

Yet what could they say in 1987 when a Sacramento couple packed their bags in the middle of the night, drove to Placerville and reported to the sheriff that someone was being murdered in the next room? Investigators subsequently found nothing.

Frank, a retired sheet metal worker and avowed skeptic, was bar tending one night when two wine glasses slid across the bar on their own—as though moved by unseen hands.

That night the staff gathered after closing as Frank and Darlene sat down with a Ouija across their knees. After nearly a half hour of concentration, the Ouija pointer began to move indicating a spirit presence. "Who are you?" Darlene asked.

Moving from letter to letter the pointer spelled out the name G-E-O-R-G-E. The assembled group asked a variety of questions. Answers were chatty and a tad mischievous—not too surprising when the spirit at last explained that he was only two years old.

But that's not the end of the story. Two days later Kay Morton, a Placerville artist, had dinner at the Vineyard House with a group of friends. It was her first visit.

At dinner, Morton says, she felt the presence of a small boy who asked her to mash his carrots and give him a cracker. Her companions saw nothing, but later in the evening Morton asked the bartender, Patty Backhaus, if there was a very small boy named George living in the house. Backhaus, who'd watched the Ouija activity, nearly dropped the drink she was serving.

Louise & Robert Chalmers are buried in this pioneer graveyard across the street from the Vineyard House.. Photograph by C.J. Marrow.

Kay Morton, unable to get the experience out of her mind, returned to the Vineyard House a few days later. She wanted to walk through the building when it was quiet. Upon entering Room No. 5 on the second floor, Morton was "overcome by a sense of fear and pain." "It was," she said, "as if spirits were trying to get out of the room."

Frank and Darlene could only look at one another in shocked disbelief. Room No. 5 was the same room where the Sacramento couple had heard sounds of the phantom murder.

Enough already! The Vineyard House closed. It remained dark and silent for years. Then in 2000 it was purchased as a private home. The brave new owners haven't seen a single ghost—yet.

The Vineyard House, now a private residence, is located off Highway 49 and Coldsprings Road in Coloma.

The Mother Lode Country/The Sierra

NEVADA COUNTY HISTORICAL MUSEUM

"THE EQUIPMENT OF THE NEVADA COUNTY FIRE DEPARTMENT is not to be excelled by that of any similar organization in any town of the same size on the Pacific Slope. The town is well supplied with hydrants and the water pressure is strong enough to throw a stream over the highest buildings."

Nevada County Historical Museum

The Nevada City Transcript had good reason to boast that March morning in 1877. A well equipped fire department meant life itself to the tinderbox towns of the Mother Lode.

Firehouse No. 1 had been built in 1861. The Victorian bell tower and gingerbread trim were added a few years later. The facility continued in use until 1938. Ten years later it was converted into a museum by the Nevada County Historical Society.

But the excitement was by no means over. As antiques and artifacts arrived—so did something else. Something with an ornery desire to push people around.

Hjalmer E. Berg, then director of the museum, reported inexplicable footsteps and cold air currents. "Many times I've been in the museum but known that I wasn't alone," he says.

Once Rebecca Miller, former president of the historical society, tried to shut a cabinet door. "As fast as I could close the door, it would fly back open," she recalls. "Finally I said aloud, 'Stop this, I don't have time! ' "It stopped, but then I heard footsteps behind me. I turned, but there was no one there." (Surely a classic case of a ghost having the last word.)

Berg tells of a time when a Jesuit priest and two graduate students were touring the otherwise empty museum. They ascended the stairs to the second floor and returned almost immediately. "Are you playing a joke on us?" the priest asked. It seemed that a red-haired "floozy" in old fashioned finery had

Hjalner E. Berg. Photograph by C.J. Marrow.

startled them by appearing out of nowhere, sitting down at the piano a relic from an old whorehouse—and began to plink away.

"It didn't help at all to tell him that we had no such woman employed at the museum — which, of course, we don't. The idea of a spectral volunteer was even more alarming than a prostitute."

Another time a group of Business and Professional Women were visiting the museum. They'd examined everything on the first level and had just climbed the stairs to the second floor when all of a sudden one woman began to scream. "They're after me!" she shrieked, running down the stairs and out the front door. No one was ever able to learn what had frightened her so."

Carrigan, Irish miner. Photograph by C.J.

One of the most interesting features within the museum is an 1880 photograph of an Irish miner named Carrigan. The subject is a mature, white-bearded man, but to the side of the photograph is the image of a boy of about twelve.

According to the story, Carrigan told the astonished photographer that as the picture was taken he was thinking rather nostalgically of his boyhood. It would seem that these thoughts somehow transmitted themselves to the film, emerging as his own youthful countenance. As the years pass the boy seems to be growing clearer. Some see other faces in the photograph as well.

The late Nick Nocerino, a medium, hypothesized that these other faces are Chinese ghosts. Nocerino came to the museum at Berg's request to exorcise the place when the phenomena seemed to be taking on a more hostile character.

Both men believed that the evil influence was emanating from the thousand year old Taoist shrine at one end of the museum. The shrine had been taken from a Grass Valley joss house — joss meaning god — and is believed to be the oldest of its kind in North America.

Photograph by C.J. Marrow.

As visitors to the museum stood in front of the shrine, many experienced the sensation of being pushed or shoved. A few said they felt as if someone was trying to trip them.

Attendance at the museum was dwindling and Berg—proud of the historic displays he'd worked so hard to accumulate—was concerned.

Nocerino was able to tune in psychically to the situation, making contact with two Chinese spirits who admitted that they had been tripping pagans who got too close to their sacred altar.

Nocerino performed an exorcism ceremony to dispatch the ghosts. Berg put up a rail to discourage the guests. Between the two of them, things are back to "normal" at the museum.

The Nevada County Historical Museum is located on Main Street in Nevada City. Telephone: (530) 265-5468

The Mother Lode Country/The Sierra

LANEY HOME

ANITA AND FRANCIS LANEY LIVE IN A MARYSVILLE VICTORIAN manor house that looks like a frosty pink wedding cake. The architectural confection seems like the antithesis of the Charles Addams haunt—yet a whole family of spirits resides there.

The Laney House. Photograph by C.J. Marrow.

The Laneys bought the place in 1962, little dreaming what was in store for them. "The previous owners had no contact whatsoever with anything supernatural," Anita says. "Three years passed uneventfully. Then we began to be aware of a presence in the house. I'd come in the back door and hear music. 'Who left the stereo on?' I'd wonder. The answer was—no one. The stereo wasn't on. The music was coming from another world.

"Then the Republican women wanted to have a tea at the house. I came home from the office to get the kitchen cleaned up for them. I was rushed and not in the best mood when I heard a man's footsteps behind me. I thought, 'Oh, hell!' certain that it was my husband wanting lunch.

"'What are you doing here?' I asked without turning. There was no answer, yet I could feel someone standing just behind me. When I turned at last I found that the kitchen was empty."

One night Anita switched off the bedside lamp and settled back, only to be confronted by the head and shoulders of a man floating above the marble-topped dresser. She turned the light back on and it was gone, turned it off again and this time saw a full length form of a man.

"I knew exactly who it was," Anita says. "Norman Abbott Rideout— first owner of the house. I recognized him because he's a younger version of his father, Norman Danning Rideout, the prominent Gold Country banker of the last century—I'd seen his picture many times. I knew that the elder Rideout had built the house as a wedding gift for his son in 1885.

"Eleven years later the young husband and father was the sole victim in a mine disaster. I'm certain that it's this man whom I saw then and have seen again many times over the years."

The Laneys believe that the house is haunted not only by Norman but by his wife and children as well. "We hear their voices and footsteps often and sometimes catch glimpses of them as well," Francis explains. "There's a little boy and a pretty little girl with long blond hair—she resembles her grandfather."

"Norman and his wife are very fashionably dressed," Anita adds. "She's quite beautiful. I see her standing at the window often. They seem like such a happy family. Maybe that's why they stay here; possibly they're living out the happy times they shared in this house. It reminds me of the ghost in Our Town who came back to relive one day. Maybe they've chosen to remain here for all eternity. That would be a kind of heaven, now wouldn't it?"

Footsteps are the most common phenomenon experienced by the Laneys and their guests. One evening Anita was entertaining a branch of the American Association of University Women.

"We had just heard a review of the Edgar Cayce biography, *There Is A River,* and I was serving refreshments when we all heard the front door open," Anita recalls. "Guess the movie's out, sounds like Fran coming home," one woman said.

"But Fran didn't come in to say hello. Instead the steps went clomping on up the stairs. I called out to him and when he didn't answer I went to investigate. Nobody was there.

"Just a few minutes later a guest cried out as her spoon tore itself out of her hand and flew across the room. Somebody was there but it certainly wasn't Fran!"

The first time the Laneys heard spectral voices they were startled, but over the years have grown accustomed to them—with one exception. As Anita was bathing one morning, she heard a woman call out from downstairs. Then a man's voice answered—from right there in the bathroom. "I leaped out of the tub and grabbed a towel," Anita says. "Ghost or no ghost, I don't like the idea of a strange man in the bathroom with me!"

Anita believes that the ghosts are keeping an eye on her in more ways than one. "They have their little methods of telling me they think I'm doing too much, getting involved in too many projects. One night— morning really, it was three a. m. — I was sitting on the floor surrounded by big rolls of newsprint. Though awfully tired, I felt obligated to complete a club assignment that I'd undertaken, a decorating project.

"I heard footsteps quite clearly descending the stairs. I thought it was Fran and I was so determined to finish that I didn't say a word. The steps reached the foot of the stairs, walked down the hall and across the living room. Finally they were right behind me. I turned at last and saw—no one. Well, when it gets so bad that a ghost has to come and tell you to slow down, you begin to get the message. I got up and went to bed."

The ghosts sometimes appear a bit like animals misbehaving when their humans are away. "Once a young couple was staying in the house while we were on vacation," Anita recalls. "While sitting in the living room, they heard a terrific crash upstairs. Upon investigating, they found that two tall vases and an antique compote had fallen off a shelf.

"Our young friends were terribly upset when we got back. 'We just can't explain it,' they kept saying. I could explain it well enough. I went upstairs and said aloud, 'This doesn't please me at all. I'm very disappointed.' I left the pieces on the floor for six weeks as a kind of reminder. It hasn't happened again."

But coexisting with ghosts is a two-way street, Anita admits. "If we don't hear from them for a while, we

Anita Laney. Photograph by C.J. Marrow.

get worried. What if they should go away! Sometimes I ask, 'Are you angry with me? I'm sorry if I've done anything to displease you.' Sometimes I've even pleaded, 'Come back!'

"And they always do."

The Laney House is located at 710 D St., in Marysville.

> *Though Anita and Francis Laney no longer live in their enchanting (and possibly enchanted) Marysville Victorian, their story is just too good to leave out. I hope you've loved it as much as we do.*

The Mother Lode Country/The Sierra

CAL-NEVA RESORT

THE CAL-NEVA RESORT FLOATS ABOVE THE LAKE SPARKLING in the sun like an ivory tower. Guests crowd the crap tables and line up to play the slots, but don't let the party time atmosphere fool you. There are skeletons in the basement that go way back.

In 1926, Robert P. Sherman, a wealthy San Franciscan, built the first Cal-Neva on land taken from the Washoe Indians. Two years later Norman Blitz, known as the "Duke of Nevada," acquired the property in exchange for debts owned him. Blitz's wife was Esther Auchincloss Nash, granddaughter to the founder of Standard Oil and aunt of Jacqueline Kennedy-Onassis.

The original casino was little more than a glorified log cabin built across the California-Nevada state line. Before gambling was legal in Nevada, the canny owner shifted the tables back and forth (from "state to state") to thwart local authorities from each side.

In 1937, the Cal-Neva burned to the ground yet rose phoenix-like from the ashes. It's said that all the materials needed to rebuild the casino were stored nearby. Five hundred men were employed to work round the clock to finish the new building within a month. This is what we know today as the Indian Room, Circle Bar and main casino area.

The Cal-Neva Resort weathered heavy snowfalls and the remodeling of a succession of owners, including serious gamblers with names like "Pretty Boy," "Bones," and "Baby Face" during the 1940's and 1950's. It continued to thrive, growing bigger and more flamboyant all the time.

No owner was as famous or visible as Frank Sinatra who acquired the casino in 1960. Today visitors may tour the underground tunnel that once linked Sinatra's Cabin 5 to the hotel theater where he performed. Colin Stevens a guide, points out Cabin 4, reserved for the Kennedys, and Cabin 3 where Marilyn Monroe used to stay. He reveals the legend "A.G. 1946" on the tunnel wall which Frank is supposed to have carved. It would seem that in the 1960s Sinatra still carried a torch for his glamorous ex, Ava Gardner, and the year of their marriage.

In 1962, Frank's quick action saved Marilyn Monroe from an attempted suicide in her cabin, but only a month after her release from the hospital the actress tried again and succeeded. Guests staying in Cabin 3 have from time to time heard sobbing and smelled a lingering perfume.

Cal Neva Resort

Strange tales more frequently center around Sinatra's notorious tunnel. It's an eerie place with vestiges of rat pack glamour—the exit to the casino is still carpeted. Small wonder staff members complain of angry voices and frightful apparitions.

A controversy with the Nevada Gaming Control Board resulted in the revocation of Sinatra's gambling license in 1963. He no longer owned the casino but continued to sing there. In 1980 the casino was summarily closed; staff and patrons alike were ordered from the premises. When Charles Book reopened in 1985. food still remained on the dining tables and the kitchen was in disarray.

The Rat PAck

In 2000, with many staff members still fearful of using the tunnel, it was decided to hold a séance there. A vision of Sammy Davis Jr. was seen by some and a recording was made of unknown voices speaking a strange language. Later someone suggested that the language might be Native American.

It was decided to take the tape to a Washoe Indian living in Reno. He confirmed that the voice was indeed speaking a Washoe dialogue but refused to translate, saying instead:

"You don't want to know."

The Cal Neva Resort is located on Crystal Bay on the north shore of Lake Tahoe with the California-Nevada line running through it. Phone (800) 225-6382.

TRUCKEE HOTEL

GUESTS ARE INVITED TO "WRAP THEMSELVES IN HISTORY" AT the Truckee Hotel, a   hostelry that once boasted of being the best stagecoach or train stop-over between San Francisco and Salt Lake City. It was also considered the perfect vantage point from which to visit Lake Tahoe—then a nine hours stage ride.

A room of the Truckee Hotel

Part of the hotel's charm is that it hasn't changed much. The Truckee doesn't have TVs or even telephones. Since 1873, guests have made their own entertainment. Or someone . . . or something . . . makes it for them.

Karen Winter, who owns the historic inn, is accustomed to guests who report women's laughter and the sound of rustling gowns in seemingly empty rooms. "Why not?" she says. "The hotel was a brothel during its boomtown days." The complaints of housekeepers are another thing. They see imprints of bodies on freshly made

The Mother Lode Country/The Sierra

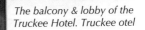

The balcony & lobby of the Truckee Hotel. Truckee otel

beds or return to find those same beds torn up. "What's that all about?"

Truckee's children are fascinated by the ghost of a man said to have broken his neck while attempting to flee a hotel fire. In 2005 a slumber party was arranged for some ghost-chasing fourth grade girls.

"I hope they won't be disappointed," a parent confided to Winter's sister, Kathryn Fisher, who'd agreed to stay with them.

"Oh, I'm sure I can arrange something," Fisher replied with a wink. Later when settling down for the night with her baby, a container of baby wipes flew off a shelf and landed at her feet.

Fisher thinks it was the ghost's way of saying. "I don't need any help from you!"

Truckee Hotel is located at 10007 Bridge St. (530) 587-4444

The Mother Lode Country/The Sierra

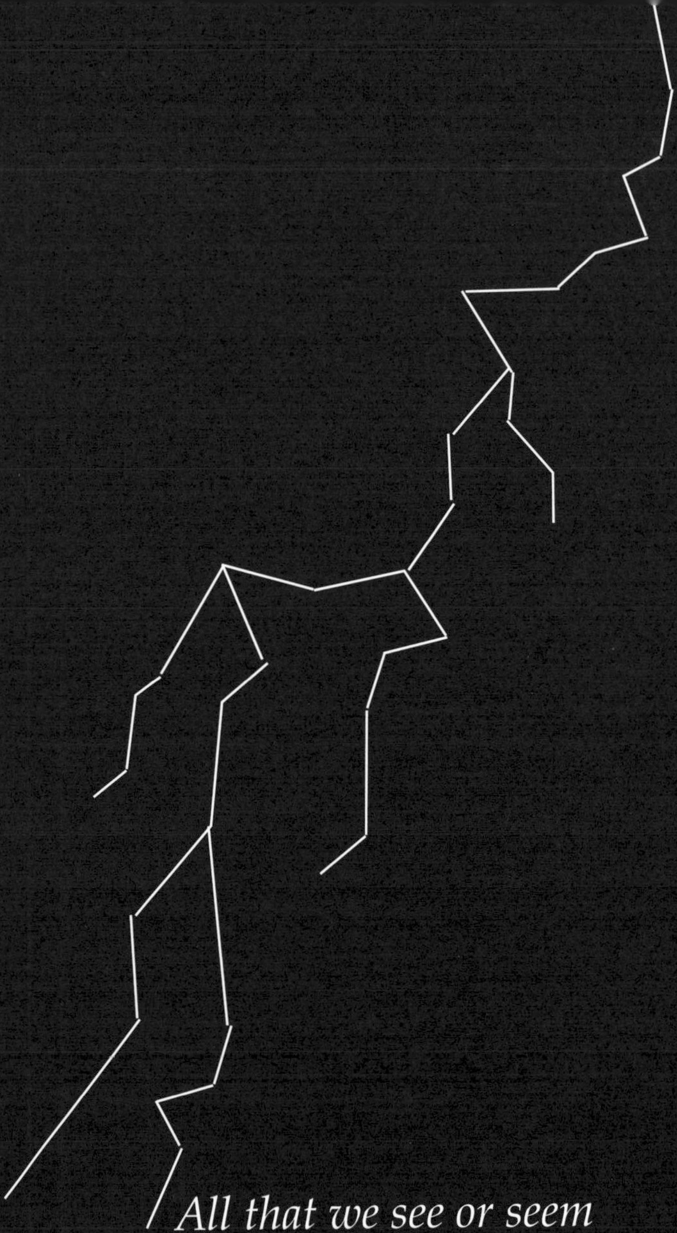

*All that we see or seem
Is but a dream within
a dream.*

—Edgar Allen Poe

CENTRAL CALIFORNIA

WINCHESTER MYSTERY HOUSE

SANTA MARIA INN

PACHECO PASS

MORGAN HILL

MOUNT MADONNA COUNTY PARK

WINCHESTER MYSTERY HOUSE

EVERY NIGHT IS HALLOWEEN AT SARAH WINCHESTER'S HOUSE.

An aura of mystery and dark foreboding surrounds the awesome structure. The towering spires, minarets and cupolas stand dark and still silhouetted against the sky. Inside there are trap doors, secret passageways and doors which open into the air.

Winchster Mystery House today. Photo courtesy of Winchster Mystery House, San Jose, CA..

The Gothic Victorian is a living monument to the dead. The legend of Sarah Winchester, who tried to shut out the grim realities of life and death with a carpenter's hammer, is everywhere.

The story of Sarah Winchester—surely the most enigmatic woman in the history of the West—is a fascinating one, as is the legend of the house itself. To the pioneers of the 19th century, the

Winchester repeating rifle was "the gun that won the West." But to Sarah Pardee Winchester, heiress to the fortune of the Winchester Repeating Arms Co., the weapon was an instrument of doom and ultimate destruction for herself.

According to the story, the widow of the rifle manufacturer's only son was informed by a Boston medium that the spirits of those killed by Winchester rifles had placed a curse upon her. The medium advised Sarah that she might escape the curse

Aerial view.. Photo courtesy of Winchster Mystery House, San Jose, CA..

by moving west and building a house. As long as the building continued, the vengeful spirits would be thwarted and Sarah would live.

The unhappy heiress obediently moved to California and purchased an eight-room farmhouse which she proceeded to remodel literally as the spirit moved her. The construction project, begun in 1884, was to occupy the next thirty-eight years of her life and would ultimately employ hundreds of artisans working on a 'round the clock basis that included Sundays and holidays.

An early addition was a tower, housing a huge bell, but with no way of getting to it except by climbing over roofs and placing ladders against the side. Inside the tower was a smooth, unscalable well, down the center of which hung the bell rope. It was through an underground passage, known only to one servant and his understudy, that the end of the rope could be reached.

The bell ringer always carried an expensive watch. Every day he telephoned an observatory and checked the correctness of his chronometers, from which, in turn, he set his watch. The bell rang

Central California

only at midnight and 2 a. m. — an occurrence that puzzled neighbors for years. Later it was learned that these were the hours when Sarah's spectral guests arrived and departed.

Design conferences took place in the seance room where the lady of the house retired each night. Just before midnight Sarah donned a gown etched with occult designs to prepare for her nightly seance. After slipping through her Victorian labyrinth, she pressed a button, and a panel slid open enabling her to step quickly from one apartment to the next. Following yet another maze, she came to the Blue Room with its thirteen coat hooks and emerged just as the bell tolled twelve.

For the next two hours she would await ghostly instructions. Her spectral consultants were capricious and insatiable, demanding room after room, balcony after balcony, chimney after chimney. The strange growth spread until it reached a distant barn, flowed around and adhered to it like a tumor, and finally engulfed it. An observation tower shot up, only to be choked by later construction until nothing could be seen from it.

To the original eight rooms, hundreds were added, many of them quickly ripped out to make way for new ideas from Mrs. Winchester's nocturnal advisors. Today, one hundred and sixty rooms of this baffling labyrinth still stand, the survivors of an estimated seven hundred and fifty chambers interconnected—if one can use that term—by trick doors, self intersecting balconies and dead-end stairways.

Literally miles of winding, twisting, bewildering corridors snake through the house while numerous secret passageways are concealed in the walls. Some end in closets, others in blank walls. The door from one was the rear wall of a walk-in icebox. The halls vary in width from two feet to regulation size and some ceilings are so low that an average size person must stoop to avoid bumping his head.

The explanation for all this is that the house was devised by ghosts for ghosts. If ghost stories are to be believed, spirits dearly love to vanish up chimneys. So Sarah obligingly provided them with not one but forty- seven of these escape hatches.

The lonely widow was obviously in-triqued by the number thirteen as well as by other aspects of the occult. Nearly every column in the house—from the ma-hogany newell post inlaid with rosewood in the hallway to the uprights supporting the porch roof—was carefully inverted and installed upside down. The interior courtyard contained a hedge cut into the ancient half moon symbol. Sarah's green-house had thirteen cupolas, there were thirteen palms lining the driveway, thir-teen lights on the chandeliers, ceilings with thirteen panels, rooms with thirteen windows, thirteen bathrooms, and thir-teen drainage holes in the kitchen sink.

Sarah Winchster. Photo courtesy of Winchester Mystery House, San Jose, CA.

Whenever possible the number thirteen seems to have been incorpo-rated or its multiples (26, 39, 52). There are even thirteen parts to Sa-rah's will —yes, her signature appears thirteen times!

Dining in splendor with her secretary-companion, Mrs. Winchester frequently enjoyed the best vintage wines. One evening she went to the wine cellar—to which only she possessed the key—to locate a special bottle. To her horror, she discovered a black handprint on the wall. That night the spirits confided that it was the print of a demon's hand. Sarah took this as a warning against alcohol and had the cellar walled up so thoroughly that, to this day, the liquid treasures have never been found.

The seance room where Sarah received her instructions was off limits to other humans. Those entering the forbidden sanctuary after

Central California

her death found only a small blue room furnished with a cabinet, armchair, table, paper and planchette board for automatic writing.

The capricious mistress of the manor indulged her whimsey by never sleeping in the same bedroom for two consecutive nights. In this way she hoped to confuse unwanted spirits, but it was her servants who were confused after the 1906 earthquake. Following the severe tremor it took the staff nearly an hour to finally locate their frightened mistress who had been trapped inside a room when the wall shifted, jamming the door.

Sarah believed the terrifying experience had been inflicted upon

her as a punishment for her extravagance in constructing the front of the house. To placate the spirits, she ordered the front thirty rooms sealed off and never used. This included the grand ballroom which had been built at a cost of $9000 and a stained glass window costing $2000. The exorbitantly priced front door was used by only three people — Sarah Winchester and the two carpenters who installed it.

The ballroom at the Winchester Mystery House. Photograph by Joe Melena.

Yet money was hardly a concern. In addition to an initial inheritance of $20 million, Sarah had received 48.8 percent of Winchester Repeating Arms Company stock, giving her an income of $1000 a day (tax-free until 1913).

Despite all her efforts, death came to Sarah Winchester on September 5, 1922. Today one can still see half-driven nails where the carpenters stopped when word came that the eighty-five year old recluse had died quietly in her sleep.

The widow spent more than $5.5 million to please her discarnate friends. Unless ghosts are unspeakable ingrates, Mrs. Winchester should have been well received on the other side.

But was that the end of the story? Hardly, to judge from the weird tales surrounding the house. Over the years a variety of psychic phenomena have been reported—chains rattling, door knobs turning by themselves, windows and doors opening and closing by themselves, whispers, footsteps—a Gothic thriller seemingly come to life.

One day Sue Sale, the office manager, took a standard tour of the house. As she passed the kitchen door, Sale saw a small gray-haired lady sitting at a table. Afterwards she enquired about the tour guide in costume. "There isn't anyone in costume," she was told.

Strange circumstances have centered twice around Allen Weitzel, director of food merchandise. One evening Weitzel carefully locked all the doors to the Winchester gift shop, then went to the storeroom to turn on the alarm system. When he returned to the gift shop he found the door leading to the courtyard unlocked. He was alone in the building at the time.

Another time Weitzel walked the entire tour route shutting off the house lights. After locking up, he walked out to the parking lot, then turned to look back at the house. It was black. Weitzel proceeded across the street to his car. As he started to drive away, he looked up to see the entire third floor ablaze with light.

A man in overalls seems a prosaic kind of ghost yet he's said to return again and again to haunt the premises. Early one morning the overall-clad apparition was seen by a restoration painter, Jack Stubbert and his son, John, in the back hallway. The specter stared back at them then climbed a flight of steps half way down the hallway. When Jack and John approached the stairway the ghostly workman faded away.

Central California

Shortly afterwards, Devon Grover, a tour guide, was pointing out the basement furnace when a man wearing overalls appeared pushing a cart toward the coal chute. When he looked again the man had disappeared.

In 2000 Allison Paker, a marketing clerk, was taking an Arizona film crew through the house. As they walked past one of Sarah Winchester's infamous bathrooms with a window in the door, Paker glanced in and saw a little bottle of Vick's cough syrup on the bottom shelf. The bottle looked like an antique that might have been used in Sarah Winchester's time.

The next day Paker and the film crew walked down the same hall. Again she looked in and saw the bottle, but this time it was on the top shelf. Later that day she asked the tour administrator if someone had been cleaning in that bathroom who might have moved the bottle. She was told that no one had been in there and the door is kept locked.

One January day as Paker was getting ready to go home she dropped by the main office to turn in some papers. It was after five and dark, and she assumed the office staff had left for the day. Upon entering the main office, she looked through the opposite

door into the conference room. The light was on and the darkness outside created a mirror effect on the window. Paker saw a reflection of a person walking across the room. She went in to say hello but found no one there. Since the main office and conference room are on the second floor there's no way someone in the courtyard below could have cast a shadow on the glass.

Sylvia Browne at the Winchester Mystery House. Photograph by A. May

In order to investigate these claims, the Nirvana Foundation obtained permission to spend a night in the house. There were five in our party: the medium Sylvia Browne and her then husband, Dal; Dick Schaskey, head of the photography department at San Jose State University; Ann Fockelmann, a research associate at the foundation; and me.

Throughout the long night Sylvia, Ann and I saw moving lights for which we could not account. All of us felt sudden gusts of icy wind and cold spots. While sitting in the bedroom where Mrs. Winchester died, Sylvia and I saw great balls of red light that seemed to explode before us.

Sarah Winchester—Photograph taken by a gardener. Reprinted courtesy of the WInchest Mystery House, San Jose, CA.

As the rest of us sat on the floor of the bedroom clutching our clipboards and cameras, Sylvia saw a couple whom, she claimed, watched us intently from across the room.

During the thirty-eight years that Sarah Winchester resided in the "mystery house," her servants and other employees remained

Central California

fiercely loyal, defending her every eccentricity.   They described her as strong- minded and firm, but always fair and kind.   Each was well paid and some were rewarded with lifetime pensions or real estate.

In death, it would appear that Mrs. Winchester received the same attention from her servants as when she was alive. "The man and woman that I see are dressed in clothing popular during the turn of the century," Sylvia explained. "They're caretakers, I think. Their attitude isn't really menacing but they are watching us very carefully. They don't seem to like strangers in their house."

As the night wore on the frightening sense of being observed did not diminish. We sat for about an hour watching a ghostly shadow play across the dark walls. Each of us tried to explain the spectral light show in earthly terms. Moonlight? There was no moon. Passing cars? The few windows faced onto a dark courtyard. There were no cars.

It was a very long night.

 A daylight bustle had settled over the place as we wearily carried out our equipment the next morning. Maintenance of so large a structure never stops. The sounds one hears during the day are anything but spectral.   The carpenter's hammer echoes just as it did during the mansion's heyday.

So it would seem that Sarah Winchester does, indeed, live on as her home does—achieving its own kind of immortality.

The Winchester House, located at 525 South Winchester Blvd. just off I-280 in San Jose, is open to visitors every day but Christmas. Daily guided tours are offered and special events planned on Halloween and on every Friday the 13th. Telephone: (408) 247-2000.

SANTA MARIA INN

THE CAPTAIN WAS DASHING, HIS MISTRESS BEAUTIFUL. THE makings of a most romantic story. Too bad it turned tragic. One night the captain, anticipating a warm reception, paid a surprise midnight visit to his lady in Room 221. He discovered her lying lifeless across the bed. At least that was the captain's story. Only one fact was known for certain. Someone had brutally strangled his mistress.

The tragedy is said to have occurred soon after the Santa Maria Inn opened in 1917. Situated half way between Los Angeles and San Francisco, the hostelry with its 24 bedrooms and 24 baths was considered state-of-art. Over the years, many celebrity guests, including Marion Davies and William

Santa Maria Inn

Randolph Hearst, Joan Crawford and Clark Gable, Mary Pickford and Douglas Fairbanks, found it the perfect place for a rendezvous.

Despite her bad luck, the captain's lady seems to agree. She's still reluctant to leave the party. Numerous guests have reported seeing her form floating over the bed in Room 221. Others in nearby rooms have complained of hearing the sounds of loud revelry or even screams coming from 221 when the room was known to be unoccupied.

Guests are not alone in experiencing strange activity. Angel Bourbon, the inn's long time bartender, recalls nights when he's

Central California

heard the sound of piano music from behind locked doors. Upon obtaining a key and entering, the room was empty.

One evening Ryan Smith, the inn's reservation supervisor, was asked get a rollaway bed for a guest. As he stepped inside the fifth floor storeroom, the door unaccountably slammed shut behind him. A cold chill filled the room. Fortunately, the door hadn't locked. After delivering the bed, he decided to take the elevator down to the lobby. When Ryan reached the elevator, the doors were open and waiting for him. Normally the elevator rests on the lobby floor, doors closed until summoned.

Ryan experienced yet another strange phenomenon. Called to a guest's room to exchange a clock that wasn't working, he saw the hands spinning wildly. When he picked up the clock, the hands moved forward in an orderly fashion, stopping at the exact time.

Another evening manager, pausing in the kitchen to get a cup of coffee, was alarmed to see the oven doors opening and closing by themselves. Late one night Chef Jacques heard a piano playing behind closed doors in the ballroom. When he entered, the music stopped abruptly. The ballroom was empty.

Housekeepers doing their regular room inspection have entered empty rooms to find furniture mysteriously stacked in corners with no explanation of how it got that way. One woman, performing tasks on the second floor, had a balloon follow her from room to room, then float above her head down the stairs to the first floor.

Still another time a housekeeper was making up the bed in the infamous Room 221 when she felt an icy hand on her shoulder. The woman turned, felt enveloped in chilling coldness and fled the building—not even stopping for her paycheck. She has never returned.

Santa Maria Inn, 801 South Broadway, Santa Maria. (805)-928-7777.

PACHECO PASS

RESIDENTS AND OFFICIALS OF SANTA CLARA AND SAN BENITO counties routinely urge the rerouting of treacherous Highway 152, the road that has claimed the lives of nearly 200 people in the past decade alone.

Pacheco Pass, the heavily traveled highway through the Coast Range between Los Banos and Gilroy, has a history of tragedy that reaches back nearly two centuries. In the early 1800s, the Indians called the Pacheco pass the "Trail of Tears," for it was their avenue of escape from the harsh rule of Father Felipe Arroyo who held them enslaved at Mission San Juan Bautista. Many of his "neophytes," unlucky enough to be caught were beaten and dragged back in chains to the mission by the Spanish padres who depended upon them for a cheap labor force to maintain their feudal empire. *Casa de Fruta,* now a popular tourist attraction, marks the site of an artesian well where the Indians once stopped to refresh themselves before beginning the hazardous trek.

The pass gets its name from the Francisco Pacheco family who received it in 1843 as part of a 150,000 acre land grant. It was thought by the Mexican government that the presence of Don Francisco, a gun carriage maker, might be a deterrent to Indians — freed at last from bondage by the secularization of the missions — who resented the settlers now pouring into their land.

But Indians weren't the only menace to new arrivals. With the Gold Rush came the bandits, Joaquin Murieta and Tiburcio Vasquez among the most notorious. In 1851 Pacheco moved his family from "the wilds" to Monterey. The violence remained. And, if anything, the coming of "civilization" only intensified it. Cars began to navigate the winding pass in the 1920s and soon

Central California

the unprecedented accident rate caused the area to be known as "blood alley."

One of many eerie tales told about this ominous stretch of highway is that of a woman who was struck by a semi-truck as she was walking along the side of the highway. Over the years motorists have professed to see her in the passenger seat of the truck. She is screaming in terror. Invariably, the woman and the phantom truck slowly disappear.

Other ghost tales recall the 19th Century when the Pacheco Pass was a stagecoach road connecting Santa Clara Valley to the San Joaquin Valley. There have been many sightings of a woman dressed in Victorian clothing searching for her lost child. Witnesses of this apparition hear the thundering rumble of a stagecoach rolling by and horses snorting.

Sylvia Browne tells of the time she and her then husband, Dal, were returning from a short vacation at Palm Springs on January 30, 1977. It was 6:30 p. m. and they had just reached Pacheco Pass on Highway 152.

They were passing San Luis Dam when unaccountably their good humored banter ceased. Sylvia felt suddenly overcome with anxiety. As a lifelong medium, she has had countless brushes with the supernatural, but nothing comparable to this wave of sheer panic.

Sylvia glanced at her husband. He seemed oblivious to the turmoil that had enveloped her so completely. "This is what hell must be," she thought and started to pray. But prayer only increased Sylvia's discomfort; she could recall nothing beyond, "Our Father." It seemed now that hundreds of voices were assailing her consciousness, strident, angry voices without words. Sylvia felt that she had been plunged into an endless void of pain and terror which seemed to have no beginning and no end.

"Help me!" she gasped, clutching Dal's arm.

"What is it, honey, tell me?"   Later she learned that he had repeated the words again and again, finally shouting them when she failed to respond. Sylvia had never heard him answer.

Dal, unable to pull off the road, continued to drive. Her sense of terror increased as images began to appear. She saw a little girl in a covered wagon cowering with her fists pressed against her eyes while Indians raged around the wagon train. Her sense of hopelessness was overwhelming. Scenes from a series of battles followed involving Spaniards, Mexicans, American settlers—all passing before her eyes in brutal succession.

"Those visions seemed to possess me, reason was useless," she said later. "Finally, as we reached the restaurant, Casa de Fruta, they began to subside, but an intense depression replaced them.

"In an effort to reach out, I talked endlessly of the experience to my family and associates at the Nirvana Foundation. They were inclined to write it off as a psychic impression — well, I've had *those* all my life. It was more than that, it had to be. Somewhere along the lonely stretch of highway known as Pacheco Pass lurks something very real, very negative and very dangerous."

The intensity of Sylvia's impressions led her to believe that others must have shared the same experiences. The flood of stories that followed her lectures confirmed this suspicion. The following are quotations taken from affidavits filed with the Nirvana foundation:

> *"In many years of going over the Pacheco Pass there has always been a deep feeling of desperate anticipation that something was going to happen to me. Also, I would have the most awful thoughts of death."*

*   *   *

Central California

"I felt totally lost and I didn't care about anything, but there was a very strong sense of fear. I knew I shouldn't be scared. . .but I can't even explain how I felt other than to say lost, panicked, and very dizzy."

* * *

"While traveling Pacheco Pass as a passenger on a very rainy night I became extremely frightened about going around the curves, although the driver was driving normally, I became really excited and asked the driver to stop for no apparent reason. We stopped and I became even more excited; we finally drove on and the feeling subsided."

* * *

"Saw lights in the sky and had a horrible feeling of being trapped. My husband was asleep and I felt

* * *

"The drive up Interstate 5 was boring and uneventful. However the ride from I-5 to highway 101, on Pacheco Pass was a nightmare I never want to relive. I have been driving for 30 years, day and night, in all kinds of weather. I have never had any fear of darkness or of driving alone. But that night on Pacheco Pass, I drove in a state of sheer panic.

"I became paranoid, feeling as if all the other cars were 'out to get me'—the ones approaching and the ones coming up behind me. I wanted to pull off the road, but couldn't. I wanted to drive slower, but seemed to be pushed and pulled by the other cars and trucks to go faster and faster. I can never remember feeling such terror for such a long period of time. I truly felt that my death was imminent."

* * *

To these, I must add my own experience. Driving the Pacheco Pass one warm September evening, I experienced total, unexplained, unaccount- able panic. Stranger yet, I couldn't get the idea out of my mind that I was being menaced by Indians. My fears began to dissipate after passing Casa de Fruta, but the depression remained for several days.

The most striking aspect of the phenomenon is this high degree of emotional involvement. All accounts refer to the anxiety experienced with no apparent cause. Sylvia Browne talks of a "nameless terror." Her intellectual control was blocked; not even simple prayers could be recalled. Terms that reappear in numerous accounts are "void," "alienated," "death," and "trapped."

Subsequent discussions with Sylvia uncovered another factor. A distortion of the local time structure seems to occur. She reports losing an hour while driving through the area. Two other persons experienced a time distortion. Their account reads:

> *"When we got to Fresno (from San Jose) and checked the time, we found that we had made the trip forty-five minutes faster than we ever had before. On the way back we lost an hour."*

* * *

An interesting point to note is that the experience occurred on January 30, 1977—the same day of Sylvia's encounter.

Sylvia believes the phenomenon is caused by an energy implant. This, she surmises, is a collection of highly charged emotional experiences that have occurred in the area. Over the years the energy from intense emotions has collected and become self-sustaining. This energy, if sufficiently strong, causes a warp in the psycho-emotional structure of space-time. The warp acts like a gravitational field, pulling other waves of emotion.

Central California

The whirling boundary can be crossed; but, once inside, the rational mind may be totally overwhelmed by negative energy. Nothing is connected to time: it is all happening now—an eternal play. The foundation of one's reality slips away leaving only a sense of utter futility.

What could have caused such an implant?

Can it be the violent history of the area—the numerous battles involving Indians, Spaniards, Mexicans, American settlers, highwaymen, and the many public hangings? Violence continues to this day in the form of numerous automobile accidents.

What obsession leads a driver to speed on a mountain highway? Could it be a compulsion to get out of there as quickly as possible? California Highway Patrol officers interviewed blamed "emotions" for many of the accidents and referred to survivors as "paranoid." A surprising number become involved in violent quarrels. An attempt to cut off or block another car may trigger a kind of war. Bumper tag may erupt into violent fist fights — or a fatal accident.

The CHP says this irrational behavior occurs frequently on the pass. One patrolman remarked. "They're all trying to die quick up there. They're all crazy."

Suicide seems to be another not infrequent cause of death on the pass. People appear to run off the edge of the road for no apparent reason. A CHP lieutenant said, "I know people who won't drive through Pacheco Pass because they're scared to death of it."

With very good reason, it would seem.

Pacheco Pass is located on Highway 152 between I-5 and Highway 101.

MORGAN HILL

MORGAN HILL'S COUPLING WITH THE AUDACIOUS HEIRESS, Diana Murphy, was the archetypical "Can This Marriage Be Saved?" saga.

Diana (who insisted that her name be pronounced Dee-awhn) was just too pretty for her own good. Born in 1859 at the pioneer Murphy family's San Martin ranch, she inherited the passionate temperament of her Spanish grandmother and the fierce Irish determination of her father, Daniel Murphy.

Nicknamed the "Duchess of Durango" (her father owned much of northern Mexico) the high spirited heiress was expelled from the Murphy-founded Notre Dame College in San Jose. She was twenty-two, had fled the ranch and

Diana Murphy-Hill as a young woman.

was living in San Francisco when she met the handsome Morgan Hill. A tall, handsome southerner with expensive tastes, Hill supplemented his earnings as a bank teller by modeling for the fashionable haberdashery Bullock & Jones.

Spirited and beautiful, Diana would have had plenty of suitors even if her father wasn't considered one of the largest landowners in the world, but Hill was "different." Older, dashing—he drove a team of mixed trotters and the finest carriage money could buy—Morgan Hill very soon cut out all the competition.

Central California

Diana Murphy-Hil

Diana's close-knit Irish Catholic family was horrified. Morgan was considered "fast." He was poor by their standards, a Protestant and eleven years older than their spoiled darling. Diana wasn't about to take "no" for an answer. In June 1882, while yachting in Santa Cruz harbor, Morgan Hill proposed marriage and Diana accepted. One month later the couple was secretly married by a Methodist minister in San Francisco.

Later that year in Nevada, Daniel Murphy was stricken with pneumonia after attempting to round up cattle in a blinding snowstorm. Diana was summoned to her father's deathbed. "Promise me," he pleaded, "that you will never marry Morgan Hill." "Yes," she whispered.

Later, overcome with guilt at the deception, Diana sought a divorce on the grounds that her father was haunting her. She was persuaded against it. On July 31, 1883, one year after their wedding date, Diana and Morgan set off for a delayed honeymoon in Paris.

Many speculated that the trip was meant to put as much distance as possible between the newlyweds and a growing scandal involving Morgan's audacious sister, Sarah Althea Hill. Sarah was recovering from an engagement to a young San Francisco attorney that had ended dramatically when she attempted to swallow a lethal dose of laudanum in his law office.

The notorious libertine, Nevada Senator William Sharon, was connected to the firm.   No one was surprised when the 60-year-old widower invited the 23-year-old beauty into his office to advise her on investments.

Known as "King of the Comstock Lode," Sharon's properties included the Palace Hotel and Grand Hotel in San Francisco. Smitten by Sarah's beauty, he struck a deal with her. If she agreed to live with him, he would pay her $500 a month. The sweetener was that he would sign a marriage contract affirming their relationship, on the condition that the document would be kept secret for two years.

Sarah settled into rooms at the Grand Hotel connected by a second story "bridge of sighs" to the Senator's rooms at the Palace. The liaison lasted fifteen months.   Then a disillusioned Sarah charged her faithless protector with "palimony."   Waving her document, Sarah brought suit: Sharon vs. Sharon. Senator Sharon counter sued.   Sharon vs. Hill.   Sarah, already flamboyant, was accompanied to court by her mentor, the notorious Mammy Pleasant, said to be a voodoo queen.

It got uglier and uglier. The Hills extended their wedding trip. A daughter, Diane, was born to them in Paris. The family remained there eight years, returning at last in 1891.

Upon her father's death, Diana had inherited 4,900 acres of the original Rancho Ojo de Agua de Coche. Social exiles from San Francisco, the couple established a country estate on the ranch property conveniently situated between Monterey Road and the Railroad tracks. Their home, designed in the popular Queen Anne style, was surrounded by orchards.

Diana created a showplace and named it Villa Mira Monte. She was proud of the hand crafted doorknob fashioned after the popular Gilbert and Sullivan operetta, *The Mikado.*   The Tiffany-inspired stained glass windows adorning the front doors

Central California

Villa Mira Monte

were carved with the initials "MH" set inside roundels beneath.

Before long curious San Francisco socialites were taking the train south to see this wilderness mansion for themselves. In those days trains stopped on request. Guests asked to be let off at "Morgan Hill's." The outings became popular. The estate was grand, the Hills' daughter, Diane, a little princess even prettier than her mother. Unfortunately life was not so sanguine between Morgan and Diana. Who knows, perhaps Daniel's spirit continued to haunt his disobedient daughter. The Hills separated. Morgan moved to the Murphy ranch near Elko, Nevada. Diana and Diane roved restlessly between San Francisco, Washington, D.C., and Paris.

In 1892, the Morgan Hill ranch property was subdivided and sold in 10 to 100 acres parcels. Streets were laid out for a township and businesses established. The City of Morgan Hill was incorporated on November 2, 1906.

By now, Diane had made her Washington debut as Diane Murphy-Hill. Diana was determined that her daughter would marry royalty but Diane was equally adamant that she would rather marry an "honest farmer." In 1911, the 27-year-old Diane gave in. She became the bride of Hardouin de Reinach-Werth, a young French baron. To everyone's surprise, Morgan and Diana Hill were the only witnesses.

The newlyweds set off for a honeymoon in Europe. Morgan returned to the Nevada ranch. Diana remained in Washington. While in Paris, the bride received word that her father had suffered a stroke. Before she could join him, Diane had a nervous breakdown. While hospitalized, she flung herself out the window and was killed on the cobblestones below.

Morgan never recovered. After his death in 1913, his remains were brought to the Santa Clara Catholic cemetery where he was interred beside Daniel Murphy, the father-in-law who never accepted him. It's hard to imagine that either of them rests easily.

Diana, nothing if not resilient, forged a place for herself in London society. She was presented at court and married Cecil Rhodes. Diana never returned in life to Morgan Hill, yet few who visit Villa Mira Monte—now a museum—doubt that her spirit is very much a presence there.

With so many restless souls rooted in Morgan Hill, is it any wonder that the whole town seems haunted? Consider the popular Golden Oak Restaurant. Built in 1934 as a working winery, the building is constructed of handmade bricks and redwood milled in the Santa Cruz Mountains.

Darlene Guevara, who manages the restaurant, was working upstairs late one summer afternoon in 2005 when she saw someone dart by the open door. "You can come out now," she called, but no one answered. Finally Guevara got up to investigate. There was no one else upstairs nor could anyone have

Central California

descended the steep, narrow stairway without her hearing. She was alone, but for the strong, lingering scent of cigarette smoke.

Later Guevara and another employee decided to consult a Quija Board. They succeeded in contacting the spirit of a nine-year-old who'd drowned in the cellar, once used as a holding tank for wine. The entity claimed to have been kidnapped. So far the story has not been verified.

Hector Hernandez, a bus boy, has twice seen a spectral guest seated at Table 11 when the restaurant was closed. A foggy form has appeared to two customers, Gil Thomas and Jeff Kahn. The bar, too, has more spirits than one bargains for. David Mito, the bartender, tells of glasses that jump off the shelf and an elderly lady seen by several guests watching them from a high wall—accessible to mortals only by ladder.

Scramblz restaurant

Jennifer Amville, an accountant, walked through one afternoon with her four-year-old son, Jake. "Who's that man in the chair?" he asked, pointing to an empty bar stool. "What's his name?" There was no one there—no one that Jennifer could see, at least.

The lively *Scramblz Diner,* a very modern eatery in a former Victorian home, reports poltergeist activity. Patrons and guests alike have seen plates and glasses literally fly off the shelves and a cash register so eager that it springs open by itself.

The *Morgan Hill Times* also has a ghost. Passersby see a spectral form at the window thought to be the ghost of a woman who lived in the upstairs apartment during the 1960s. Her son, a middle school student, returned one afternoon to find his mother dead of a heart attack.

Seems ghosts are so common in this town that residents take them for granted. Raymond and Jacquelyn Keith lived with theirs for forty-three years. Time after time the couple saw a young girl, of about thirteen, in high button shoes and an old fashioned dress. The Keiths wondered if she wasn't in some way tied to the land rather than to their house, for Central Avenue had once been a thoroughfare for wagon trains. Nevertheless, it was their Victorian home that realtors considered haunted. The couple had to sign a disclosure form before the house could be sold.

Villa Mira Monte, 17860 Monterey Rd. Hours: Friday from 12 to 3 p.m. and Saturday from 10 a.m. to I p.m. Phone (408) 782-7191.

Golden Oak Restaurant, 15595 Condit Rd. Phone: (408) 779-8085

Scramblz Diner, 775 East Dunne Ave. Phone: (408) 779-0779.

Morgan Hill Times Building, 30 East Third St.

MOUNT MADONNA COUNTY PARK

IF THERE EVER WAS A SPIRIT WHO HAD REASON TO BE RESTLESS its Sarah Miller, the daughter of cattle baron, Henry Miller, and his wife. The eight-year-old was riding with her parents when her horse stumbled. Sarah was thrown to the ground and killed when the horse attempted to regain its footing.

The bereaved parents took the child to Laurel Hill Cemetery in San Francisco for burial in the family vault. A week later, deciding the location was too cold and cheerless, they moved her to a smaller cemetery closer to home on Castro Valley Road.

Miller Ruins.

Nearly fifty years later this cemetery was abandoned. Sarah was taken from beneath the tomb inscribed "Mamma's and Pappa's Pet" and returned to San Francisco. In the 1940s, Laurel Hill Cemetery was abandoned. The bodies interred there were relocated to other cemeteries.

Sarah is thought to be interred now in San Bruno's pioneer cemetery, but many over the years have seen her spectral form riding through what is now Mount Madonna County Park past the ruins of her family home. Others claim to see the ghost of her father also riding through the dense forest. Henry had wanted to be buried among the redwoods, but his wishes were ignored and he too was interred at Laurel Hill only to be later dug up and buried—who knows where.

Henry Miller's amazing story began in 1850 when, then known as Heinrich Alfred Kreiser, he emigrated from Germany with just six dollars in his pocket. For the first eight years he worked as a butcher, saving his money. By 1858, he was able to buy land and within a few years had acquired 14.5 million acres of land in California, Oregon and Nevada. A million head of cattle and 100,000 sheep grazed his land. When Miller died in 1916, his estate was worth more than fifty million dollars.

Little Sarah had loved camping with her family at their summer place which would later be named Mount Madonna. In 1879, the family enjoyed "roughing it" in brightly colored, fully furnished and carpeted tents. After Sarah's death, Miller built four houses on the site. First there was a two-story redwood cabin, then houses for each of his two surviving children. Finally in 1901, he built his grandest structure—an elaborate home with seven bedrooms and baths, a living room with a veranda on three sides and a 3,600 square foot ballroom.

Some say the Italian woodcutters employed by Miller gave the place its name: Madonna. Others believe it was a visiting poet, Hiram Wentworth.

Central California

The stairs going nowhere at the Miller Ruins.

Today the Millers' retreat—originally an Ohlone Indian hunting grounds—has   become the 3,688 acre Mount Madonna County Park. To the east, the park overlooks the Santa Clara Valley, to the west, Monterey Bay. As the slopes of Mount Madonna descend toward the valley, the landscape changes from redwood forest to oak woodland, dense chaparral and grassy meadows.

Little remains of the mountain palace. A few stone walls, a foundation and stairs that lead nowhere are a poignant but telling monument to the passing of time. One needn't see a ghost to feel that the place is haunted by the joys and sorrows of the almost legendary millionaires who came so far to be alone. Why did their grand enclave fall to ruin? Dense forest surrounds the fallen stones. The aura is disquieting but also spellbinding. It's easy to imagine Sarah and Henry returning here, easy to imagine seeing them.

Mount Madonna County Park is on Highway 152 (Hecker Pass Highway) ten miles west of Gilroy. Turn right on Pole Line Rd. Go 1.5 miles to a paved road and turn right. The ruins are 1/4 mile past the ranger station. Phone: (408) 842-2341

Central California

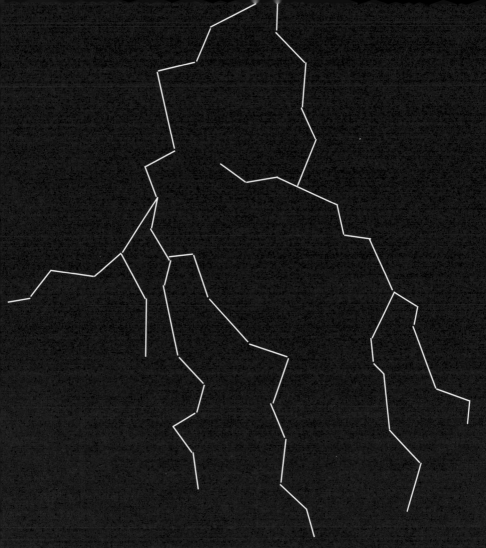

While yet a boy I sought for ghosts,
...with fearful steps pursuing
Hopes of high talk with the departed dead.
                                        —*Percy Bysshe Shelley*

CENTRAL COAST

PIERPOINT INN

STEVENSON HOUSE

STOKES ADOBE

SUNSHINE VILLA

BROOKDALE LODGE

RED, WHITE & BLUE BEACH

MOSS BEACH DISTILLERY

PIERPOINT INN

Dear Mr., Mrs., And Miss Motorist:
Wouldn't you like to find an Inn on the Bluff by the Sea?
One of those old fashioned vine covered and tree shaded
kind you read about,
With acres of trees, shrubs, flowers and lawns.

THIS QUAINT '20S PITCH WAS MEANT TO STEER MOTORISTS to the Pierpont Inn which sits majestically between Los Angeles and Santa Barbara. .

An apparition appeared to a guest staying in this cottage

The inn's tradition began with Josephine Pierpont, a Chicago socialite who'd moved to the area for her husband's health. Horseless buggies were all the rage and canny Josephine sensed that the time had come for a modern inn that would cater to travelers motoring the Pacific coastline. Besides, her son, Austin, was about to graduate from Stanford. Wasn't this just the project to keep him occupied?

The inn was designed in the then popular Arts and Crafts style by Sumner P. Hunt, the area's premier architect, and completed in 1910. Austin took over but by 1915, he'd decided to become an architect himself and took off to Los Angeles. In the mid 20s, Austin came back with big ideas of turning the inn into a country club. During that time he added two Tudor cottages to the Craftsman complex.

The Country Club venture was not a success. Austin drifted on to another project and, in 1928, the inn was sold to Mattie Vickers Gleichmann. Mattie was a high school teacher who'd fallen madly in love with Gus Gleichmann, a major league ball player. Gus's greatest dream was to own a hotel. He knew all about running one—"I should," he assured everyone who'd listen—"I've stayed in enough of them."

Mattie had never stayed in any but she was sure that Gus knew everything. Somehow she managed to convince her father, Ashby Vickers, of that as well. The couple borrowed $80,000 (a huge some then) from the Bank of Daddy. It was a family affair from the beginning. Mattie and Gus closed the inn for one year while in-laws and siblings showed up to scrub floors and tiles, paint walls and sand stairways. Gus's mother watched all the assorted children as they played hide and seek in the gardens.

In 1929 the inn re-opened as a grand hotel. Gus died in 1938 but Mattie continued to fulfill his dream on her own. She lived to be one hundred; and, assisted by her son, Ted, and later by his son, took an active part in running the inn to the very end of her life. Over the years the Pierpont has been a haven to Babe Ruth, Charlie Chaplin, Bette Davis, Bing Crosby, and Cecil B. DeMille. George H.W. and Barbara Bush were guests in one of the cottages for several months in 1949 when the former president was a 25-year-old oilman and his son, George W. was a boy in knee pants.

Central Coast

Even more titillating than the celebrity guests are the spectral ones. In summer of 2005, Sean, a kitchen server, reported seeing a woman wearing a satin gown with long while gloves, her dark chignon tucked under a feathered hat. The final touch was an umbrella.

Suzanne Lawrence as Josephine offers tours of the Pierpoint. Here she is shown in a hallway believed to

Kirk Benitez, the banquet manager, while carrying linens down a hallway heard the sound of women's voices laughing and chattering. Beyond a glass door he saw figures moving, women in large hats, but as he opened the door, they disappeared. Over the years Benitez has also heard the sounds of people partying in an otherwise empty room as well as children laughing in the garden when there are known to be seen.

While standing at the copy machine, Kathy Farrell-Gordon looked down the hall to see a maintenance man approaching with a tow-headed child at his side. As he drew nearer, the child disappeared. "Where did the girl go?" Kathy asked.

"What girl?" was his puzzled reply.

Sales coordinator, Christina Franklyn was checking out a meeting room when she heard thundering footsteps coming down the stairway. An outside door flew open by itself, but she saw nothing there. People have also reported loud footsteps in the Sun Room where enlisted men were quartered during World War II.

Ventura resident Bruce Barrios and a friend stopped by the Pierpont bar for a last call after a long day's work. As they sat talking, Barrios observed something strange moving out of the corner of his eye. Turning, he saw a vapor-like mist formed by three ribbon shapes gently floating above an empty table. Barrios looked back at his friend to point out what he'd seen. When he turned his head again, the mist had disappeared. The bartender who'd been standing in front of the two men was alarmed at how white Barrio's face had become.

Since neither of the other men had seen the vision, Barrios dismissed it as a figment of his imagination. However, when he and his friend went to his car and opened the door both were assaulted by the strong odor of flowers. The sweet, very heavy scent reminded each of them of a funeral. The odor was only in the car, not around it.

Many staff members over the years have reported being visited by Ted Gleichmann, who assisted his mother with the management of the hotel from the early 1950s to 1975 when he died of a brain tumor. "Ted's" specter is invariably described as a well dressed figure in a dark suit. The employees believe that he's checking on the hotel just as he did in life.

The sightings are not confined to staff members. A guest staying in one of the Tudor cottages that Austin built long ago saw a man in a bowler hat silhouetted against the wall. Later he saw two children seated on a garden bench beside an older woman. Is Gus's mom still baby sitting?

Pierpont Inn is located at 550 Sanjon Rd., Ventura. Phone: (800) 643-6144

Central Coast

STEVENSON HOUSE

BARBARA BURDICK, CURATOR OF THE STEVENSON HOUSE, a museum in the Monterey State Park, is at a loss to answer the question. The "who" remains a mystery. The "what" is for certain.

The woman in black is a ghost.

Legends are legion concerning the former boarding house now named for its most illustrious lodger, Robert Louis Stevenson. Many speculate that the "lady in black" is actually Fanny Osbourne—the alluring woman Stevenson came all the way from Scotland to woo and subsequently married.

But most—including Barbara Burdick—believe the ghost is Manuela Giradin, owner of the house during Stevenson's stay. They think the spirit of Manuela is in fact reliving the last tragic weeks of her life.

During the summer of 1879, Mrs. Girardin lost her husband, Juan, in a typhoid epidemic. Then in early December her two grandchildren fell ill of the same disease. Manuela worked desperately to save the children, tending them literally night and day. Then the devoted grandmother caught the fever from her young patients. She died on December 21st, never knowing that her grandchildren had recovered largely through her efforts.

Over the years a variety of phenomena have been observed, almost invariably during the first three weeks of December. "People from out of state who know nothing of the legend will see all kinds of things," the curator says. "A rocking chair in the nursery will suddenly begin to rock of its own accord, or they'll smell carbolic acid—often a sickroom disinfectant."

"Each year an apparition is seen. 'Isn't it nice that the housekeeper is in costume just like you?' someone will say, pointing at what appears to be a blank wall. Perhaps I wouldn't believe—not all the park employees do—if I hadn't seen her myself."

Late one foggy afternoon when Barbara Burdick was preparing to lock up, she noticed a woman in black gazing intently down at the children's bed. "She was oddly dressed in a long gown with a high lace collar, but aside from that looked as 'lively' as anyone," she recalls.

"Despite the stories, it never occurred to me that she wasn't just another tourist. When I explained that it was closing time, she nodded understandingly.

"I turned to leave and then looked back, wondering just how she had managed to get inside the barred room. The nursery was empty."

The haunted nursery in the Robert Loius Stevenson house. Photograph by C.J. Marrow.

The Stevenson House, located at 530 Houston St., is open every day but Wednesday from 10 to 11 a. m. and 1 to 4 p. m. Visitors must register for tours in advance. Telephone: (831) 649-7118.

Central Coast

STOKES ADOBE

CAN LOVE TRANSCEND THE GRAVE?

Jehanne Powers once thought so. The widow of Gallatin Powers, founder of the world famous restaurant, *Gallatin's,* Jehanne bravely continued its management until her own death. Today it is known as Stokes Adobe.

Built in 1838, the historic Stokes Adobe was once a grand mansion, the residence of James Stokes, first mayor of Monterey. Today it's an elegantly appointed dining house filled with valuable antiques.

The polished silver candelabra and exquisitely cut glass chandeliers recall a time when Monterey was the Spanish capital of California. Surely many of the appointments were in the house during the exciting days when the city was menaced by the dreaded pirate, Hippolyte de Bouchard. Others date from the tempestuous era when Monterey was besieged by American forces. Could it be an energy implant, some psychic remnant of bygone terror that continues to "haunt" the restaurant today?

Kara Caswell, Jehanne's former partner, feels otherwise. "There were two kinds of things happening when I was there," she explains. "One kind involved ghosts that people saw, the other involved things that happened. Maybe ghosts also caused the happenings--they definitely appeared to be directed by some kind of intelligence.

"Why am I so sure? Because most of the time the victims seemed chosen for a reason. We'd discover that a certain employee hadn't been quite honest. Before we could fire him, he'd quit. The stories were always the same. 'Something' seemed to be shaking him, pushing him down the stairs, or he'd hear footsteps following him about the place late at night when he knew he was all alone. It seemed like a force was literally trying to shake these people up, telling them to shape up or get out--and that's exactly what happened.

"Once we had a bartender who was cranky. He fixed drinks well enough, but customers just didn't like him. It's hard to fire someone on the basis of personality alone but that seemed the

Stokes Adobe.

only course to take. We didn't have to worry long. First he complained about glasses falling off the bar, no one paid much attention. Then one night I heard him yell. Rushing into the banquet room, I saw that the whole back bar—a massive mahogany thing—had begun to move. For a minute I thought we were having an earthquake, but everything else was still. Not so much as a single prism of crystal from the chandelier was moving. That was the last we saw of that bartender. He left immediately."

Jehanne Powers believed that something was trying to attract her attention as well. One night she and Kara had closed the empty restaurant at 3 a.m. only to have the Muzak turn itself on full force as they reached the parking lot.

Many windows opened by themselves and often every light in the place turned on—with no master switch. One night the police called Jehanne to report a light inside the restaurant and asked her to meet them there with a key so they wouldn't have to break in. Driving there, she vividly recalled turning off every light herself. Jehanne found the restaurant surrounded by police. One man took the key and went inside.

As he stood in the entry, the policeman heard the sound of steps climbing the stairs, crossing the banquet room and entering a small room off to the side. Following, he approached the open door and demanded, 'Come out with your hands up!' Suddenly the door slammed shut knocking the gun out of his hand. At last, joined by reinforcements, he tore open the door. The tiny room—which has no window or exit--was completely empty.

On another evening Kara's son, Charles, was polishing silver in the banquet room when he was startled by the sound of someone crying. Looking up, he saw the figure of a young woman in a long white dress. "I'm so sad," she said, wringing her hands.

Jehanne believed this to be the ghost of Evangeline Estrada whose sweetheart, Juan Escaba, was killed in the brief war for statehood. "It's easy to imagine that the grieving girl might remain at the scene of her romance, waiting endlessly for her lover to return," she speculated.

Again and again diners inquire about the lady in black. "Are you having a costume party upstairs?" a man asked, explaining that he'd glimpsed an older woman in a long black gown ascending the stairs. There was no costume party.

Another man felt a gown sweep the back of his chair. Turning to see if there was room for her to pass, he looked directly into the face of an older woman who seemed to melt into nothingness as she reached the stairway.

This time Jehanne believed they were seeing the ghost of Hattie Gragg, a very strong-willed woman who had lived in the house prior to her suicide in 1948. The Graggs were a proud family who had fallen on hard times. It was a tragedy for her heirs to have to sell the historic house but it was heavily mortgaged. Jehanne felt that Hattie bitterly resented seeing strangers--restaurant guests--in her home.

But Hattie Gragg's animosity toward the restaurant—and possibly herself—was not the only problem facing Jehanne Powers. "I think my husband is here too," she confided to me. "Ours was a very close, extremely loving relationship. I think he wants me with him on the other side."

Were Jehanne's suspicions correct? One can only speculate. At the time of the interview, her health was failing. She died and Gallatin's passed into the hands of another restaurant owner and then another. The ventures were not successsful. The building remained closed and shuttered for five years before reopening under a new name that's really quite old, Stokes Adobe.

And the ghost? The present owner and staff are certain that *something's* there--something nice. "Yes, we all feel a presence," Lucien Lentzinger, the host says, "but it's a welcoming one. Our guests feel it too. Perhaps all the lovers are united, all scores settled. Whatever's there, we're sure it likes us."

Central Coast

Stokes Adobe is located at 500 Hartnell Street, Monterey.

Telephone: (831) 373-1110

SUNSHINE VILLA

THE CRUMBLING VICTORIAN LOOMED EERIE AND ABANDONED atop Beach Hill for nearly a decade.

The Sunshine Villa. Photograph by Vern Appleby.

Everybody has stories about the old McCray hotel. Alfred Hitchcock once lived nearby and the McCray was said to have been the inspiration for the building in his film, *Psycho*. Herbert Mullins, who killed thirteen people including a priest in a confessional, lived in the hotel during the height of his murderous rampage. Santa Cruz police admit that after the place was closed it was the scene of satanic rituals as well as drug dealing. Historians speculate that the building rests on the bones of angry Ohlone Indians. Many say the house — now renovated and reincarnated as a retirement home — is haunted.

The strange story may have had its beginnings hundreds, perhaps thousands, of years ago when the Ohlones climbed the hill to pay grateful homage to the sun for its daily return. Most certainly rituals were performed on the hill overlooking the sea where the sun disappeared into darkness each night.

The known history of the property has its beginnings in the mid-1860s when Dr. Francis M. Kittredge climbed the hill, admired the view and decided to build a house there for his wife. The Kittredge home was a lovely place known for its beautiful gardens, but the owners moved on. There was an attempt to establish a residential hotel, but it failed.

Then along came James Phillip Smith, a millionaire, who purchased the building for his family home. It was Smith who gave the Sunshine Villa its name. A man with big ideas to match his deep pockets, he turned the house into a community showplace. Surrounded by velvety green lawns and overlooking the San Lorenzo River as well as the sea, the mansion was the site of lavish teas, balls, musicals and banquets for visiting dignitaries.

The Sunshine Villa reached its apex in Santa Cruz social history when the owners sponsored the *Venetian Water Carnival*. The river was dammed at the Beach Hill curve to form a sparkling lagoon. Electric lights—a rarity in those days—were strung along the banks to highlight the festivities. Smith picked up the tab for everything insisting upon the very best. In an era when all was elegance, when women were lovely and men dashing, the Sunshine Villa shone.

But the Smiths too moved on, a series of new owners came and went. No one remaining long. Finally the mansion was converted once again into a hotel, the McCray. A former resident and owner, Charles Kilpatrick, who lived there until he was nine and then returned in 1977 upon the death of his parents, reports seeing a ghost.

Central Coast

"I saw it for the first time when I was six," he told the *Santa Cruz Sentinel* in 1986. "It was a blue energy cloud that materialized suddenly, growing as big as a gorilla."

In 1987 the property was acquired by its present owners. After nearly two years of remodeling and major expansion, which involved lifting the old hotel off its foundation and moving it ten feet, the doors opened on the new Sunshine Villa. Sunshine Villa is an assisted living facility for senior citizens which includes a restaurant-sized dining room, an arts and crafts complex, a beauty salon, and a courtyard with a gazebo.

The face-lifted villa now resembles a charming confection rising from the grassy hillside. No traces of the delapidated McCray remain— except......

"The place is haunted," according to Yevona Thomas, the housekeeper. "I was leaning over cleaning the pool table and something cold came over me, pushing me."

Stacy Smith, a health and wellness coordinator, also reports a chilling experience. "I felt this cold presence. It was like a whisper on my neck, kind of a gentle kiss in a way. Turning, I could see nothing; but I definitely felt a presence close by."

Bonnie Sousa, who used to work nights at the Villa, recalls hearing the sound of a young woman's voice calling from the ducts of the gas fireplace used for central heating and seeing blue lights in the blackened hallway.

Jan Kertz, a Watsonville psychic, was called in to investigate the house, sensed tragedy. "There was mental illness in the old McCray.   It got so heavy that even the drug addicts were uncomfortable there. A woman was murdered in the hotel but it was covered up somehow. She's still hanging around, hoping some one will find out about it."

Kertz attributes the phenomena to an "energy vortex" located on the site. "The Indians recognized this, but they dealt with it sacredly. We must learn to do the same."

The management of the villa feel confidant they're on the right track. Any presences that might be detected are positive, protective ones, they believe — with good reason. The reconstruction job that transformed the place was completed October 16, 1989. After months of effort, the building was finally bolted down, fully operational. The next day a massive earthquake devastated much of Santa Cruz. The Sunshine Villa sustained no damage whatsoever.

The Sunshine Villa is located at 80 Front Street, Santa Cruz, 95060. Telephone: (831) 459-8400.

Central Coast

BROOKDALE LODGE

KIM GILBERT'S ONE OF THOSE GORGEOUS BLONDES WHO slink through mystery novels. Her likes spring from the the pages of Raymond Chandler, Dashiell Hammet, Mickey Spillane. Voluptuous figure, long golden hair, husky voice—she's a mystery buff's dream come true.

Kim Gilbert. Photograph by Vern Appleby.

But Kim isn't a figment of a writer's imagination. She's a real tell it like it is type whose father is a police lieutenant. A spunky lady, who wants to be a cop herself. She's also a free spirit who believes in spirits — at least one of them — because she's seen it herself.

In 1989, Kim's parents, Lee Ann and William Gilbert, bought the once famous Brookdale Lodge. The eight-acre property, nestled between Ben Lomond and Boulder Creek on Highway 9, includes 46 motel rooms, nine cabins, three cottages, 64 condominium units, a cafe, and retail shops as well as the lodge. Built in 1923, the lodge itself houses offices, a bar and the famous Brookdale Restaurant where an actual creek and waterfall cascade through the dining room.

During its heyday in the '20s, '30s and '40s, the Lodge was a getaway for the rich and famous. Joan Crawford, Tyrone Power, Howard Hughes, Henry Ford, Hedy Lamarr, President Herbert Hoover and Rita Hayworth were among the notables who signed the guest register—plus more than fifteen million not-so-famous tourists who came to eat in the restaurant featured in "Ripley's

Believe It Or Not" and to see the property often used as a backdrop for magazine shoots and Hollywood films.

Toward the end of the glitz days, some people began to stay the night on the off chance of encountering "Sarah," the niece of the lodge owner, who some fifty years ago, drowned in the creek that runs through the dining room. Then came a series of disasters. One of the original buildings burned to the ground in 1952. Five people died in the fire. There was a serious flood in 1955, then another fire. The place changed hands several times, finally standing vacant. Most recently the lodge had a reputation as a hangout for alleged drug dealers.

William Gilbert, a traffic commander and former Tenderloin District cop who had served 23 years on the San Francisco police force, put an end to that in a hurry. "We have zero tolerance for drugs," William said. "We tell people when they call for reservations that the lodge is under new management and if they're into drugs, not to come."

The Gilberts asked their daughter, Kim, to manage the lodge while they undertook the task of restoring it to its former glory. She accepted the job while attending the police academy in San Jose.

Soon after arriving at the lodge with her small daughter, Kim began to hear strange tales from locals about ghosts said to walk the halls. She learned the lodge had been owned by gangsters in the '40s and that a number of people met violent deaths there. Kim wants to be a cop, right? Everybody who has ever watched a detective movie knows that police are supposed to be, if not cynical, then at least skeptical. Kim had her skeptical number down cold. Dismissing the stories as nonsense, she nodded her head with a certain wary tolerance, "Yeah, yeah, sure........"

Then the doors started slamming — for no apparent reason. The jukebox and television began to blare — on their own. Toilet paper rolls unwound unaided simultaneously from both the men

Central Coast

and women's restrooms. Kim noticed mysterious cold spots during sweltering summer days. The scent of gardenias slowly began to waft through the lobby, down the halls, past the bar.

Morning after morning she was awakened at 3 a.m. by a voice calling her name. Then one night after a big band appearance she and the staff were relaxing in the lounge. It was 3 a.m. and they were about to call it a morning when all heard the sound of laughter in the conference room above. Many years before this had been a game room and there was still a pool table in the corner. They heard a cracking sound, then more laughter. Rushing upstairs Kim and the others found balls scattered all over the pool table. The room was empty.

Late one night when the lodge was locked and empty, she heard big band music coming from the Mermaid Room. Now a shadowy storeroom with no working electrical outlets, the room had once been notorious. It was a glass enclosure behind which male guests could watch women — each tagged with a number — cavort above them in a large pool. It was said they had only to make their selections known and their choice would soon be waiting in a tourist cabin across the road. A secret underground panel once connected the buildings. Sometimes Kim could hear the sound of laughter, the clinking of glasses.

One night, while sitting in the lounge after the bar closed at 2 a.m., she was startled by the sound of a small child running in the lobby a few feet away. Kim looked through the large double fireplace shared by both rooms and saw a little girl in a dress reminiscent of the 1940s. Assuming that it was her own child playing dress up, Kim hurried into the lobby intending to reprimand the child and take her back to bed. The room was deserted. Rushing upstairs, she discovered her daughter fast asleep.

"What I had seen was a real little girl," Kim says. "She looked like any other except for the old fashioned clothes. As I sat beside my own child's bed thinking about it, I remembered a couple who'd come to check out the lodge's wedding facilities. They'd talked of seeing a child too, a little girl that no one else saw or could account for."

Brookdale Lodge. Photograph by Vern Appleby.

That night made a believer of Kim Gilbert. The small storeroom at the back of the lodge kitchen, a room covered with weird designs said to have been drawn by devil worshippers, was no longer a vague curiosity. Kim was afraid to go in there. Soon she noticed an unpleasant smell coming from a small dark room off the banquet hall. According to the story, mobsters had been buried there.

Dining area at Brookdale Lodge.

Kim really didn't want to investigate. Instead she called the Campbell based Church of Nova Spiritus. Two ministers arrived. Carrying lighted candles, they wandered through unfinished rooms, down dusty hallways, peering into tunnels and through iron railings, all the while praying for the eviction of any evil spirits present.

The prayers apparently had a reverse effect. "If anything, they may have annoyed the ghosts," Kim admitted later. "Shortly after the failed exorcism, I awoke one morning to find wooden planks ripped off the wall in the banquet room across from that small room where the mobsters are supposed to be buried."

Kim says ghosts per se don't bother her. She speculates, "Maybe some of them were lively, party people in life and now they simply enjoy being where the action is. My parents are trying very hard to bring back the old Brookdale Lodge feeling—the good part, the glamor and the fun. We want that kind of 'spirit,' but if the good ghosts have to leave with the bad—I'd just as soon they all go. There *is* something wrong here—I feel it."

Whatever's going on certainly hasn't affected business. If anything it's helped. "Of course," she admits, "I do get a few wacko calls. They're thinking *Exorcist* I guess — Linda Blair's head spinning around. I tell them to forget it."

A look around the newly renovated property reveals no spinning heads, no blood oozing from beneath carpets, no slime dripping from the walls. Anything but! Still, one thing's certain: Ask for spirits at the Brookdale Lodge and you may get more than a shot of whiskey.

Brookdale Lodge is located at 11570 Highway 9, Brookdale, 95007. Telephone: (831) 338-6433.

Central Coast

RED, WHITE, and BLUE BEACH HOUSE

A WOMAN WITH A REPUTATION FOR GHOST CHASING CAN expect to be asked anything. But most frequently, it's "Have you ever seen one?"

The answer is "no." I haven't seen ghosts, but I've surely felt their presence.   One even accosted me at the nude beach in Santa Cruz.

It was the scariest night of my life.

It began on another, far pleasanter evening.   At a crowded Tahoe restaurant, a friend and I shared a table with another couple, Bill and Vivian Marraccino. The usual get-acquainted question, "What do you do?" led to surprises for everyone.

"Have I got a ghost for you!" Bill exclaimed when I told him that I was a writer specializing in psychic phenomena.

"There's this haunted house down in Santa Cruz—all kinds of stuff happens there. Things fly around the room, lights go on and off..."

"Tell her about the ghost," Vivian broke in.   "It's an old sailor who walks out the back door of the house and strolls about the camp grounds. He looks so picturesque in his old rain slicker and cap that a new guy—Jim Hilburn, an engineer—tried to photograph him.   Jim got quite close to what he thought was a flesh and blood, if a bit eccentric man.   Then, as he focused his camera, the old sailor faded away."

"Then there's the window," Bill picked up the narrative, "the window that doesn't exist." He explained that they and other campers at the Red, White and Blue Beach have often observed a lighted window on the hill above the water. "It really surprised me the first time," he recalls. "I couldn't remember any buildings in that area. I thought it was just a barren hillside with nothing on it.

"The next day I discovered that it *was* just a barren hillside with nothing on it."

Of course I had to investigate this one for myself. A few days later I drove to Santa Cruz intending to interview Ralph and Kathy Edwards, the owners of the house and camp grounds. Even on a sunny day the place looks like a setting for a Gothic horror story. The Coast Highway winds its way through deserted stretches of hills and sea. On a weekday in November there was very little traffic.

The nudists can't complain of peeping toms here, I noted, turning off the road at the red, white and blue mailbox. Nothing else marked the narrow offroad which could easily be missed by passing motorists.

The narrow road wound downward from the highway, twisting and turning around rolling, mound-like hills. As I approached the isolated farmhouse, I felt that I had stepped back in time a hundred years. If ever a house looked haunted, this one did. The tall, two-story structure was like some lonely sentinel, a mute survivor. Of what, I wondered: penetrating fog and sea gales certainly. But what else?

Ralph Edwards met me at the gate. He was a tall, rangy man with a taciturn manner. "I hear you have a ghost," I ventured.

"Better talk to my wife."

"You mean you never saw it?"

"I didn't say that." He turned back to his gardening.

Central Coast

Kathy Edwards proved the opposite of her laconic husband. She was full of stories—all of them frightening. "Things are relatively quiet now—those footsteps, they aren't much. They happen so often, Ralph wouldn't get any rest at night if he ran downstairs to check every time we heard them. And the doors slamming by themselves, that's nothing. They do it most every day. My perfume bottles dance around a lot and we hear the sound of crystal shattering but never find anything broken.

"But when the girls were living at home, that's when the house was *really* active. My daughters used to have a terrible time at night. Something seemed determined to shake them right out of their beds. Sometimes they'd make up beds on the floor thinking to get away from it, but there was no escape. Every time they'd pull up the covers something would yank them away. I remember Ronda was working as a medical secretary—a really demanding job that kept her very busy. Sometimes I'd hear her pleading with the bed to let her sleep.

The Edwards home at the Red, White, and Blue Beach.

"My son, Roger, didn't believe his sisters, so one night he slept in Ronda's bed. Nothing happened and he was soon asleep. Then in the middle of the night he was awakened by what he thought was an earthquake. The bed was shaking so violently that it seemed to leap right off the floor.

"Since the girls married and moved away, whatever it is seems to have shifted its attention to the first floor. People just won't stay over night in this house. We had our last guest several years ago. A young relative sleeping on the couch was awakened by a rooster crowing. He could see its outline perched on the arm of the couch at his feet. But when he turned on the light nothing was there."

The Edwardses have never kept chickens.

Kathy tells of a Navy picture of Ralph's which was hanging in the living room. One night it flew off the wall and sailed five feet before crashing to the ground with a force so great that some of the glass splinters are still imbedded in the wood. The nail that had secured the picture remains in the wall.

"If you think any of this is funny, don't laugh too loud," Kathy advised. "I told a visitor about our ghost once and he laughed at me. That skepticism didn't amuse whatever lives here one bit. Suddenly a drawer opened by itself and a baby shoe flew out and hit him on the side of the head. That stopped his laughing in a hurry.

On Thanksgiving Day of 1975, Kathy Edwards had just opened the refrigerator door when a large plant left its standard and flew toward her—a distance of some twelve feet. Her daughter prevented a serious injury by grasping the heavy pot in mid air. But the mess could not be avoided. The plant and dirt that had been in the pot crashed against Kathy and splattered the inside of the refrigerator.

Central Coast

Ronda was the target of another attack which occurred one evening with nine people present. A glass of wine sitting on the piano flew through the air and deliberately poured itself down the front of Ronda's decollete dress.

"We have our own theories about that one," Kathy says. "Perhaps the ghost was jealous. In life she may have been very flat chested—Ronda definitely is not."

One mystery that continues to plague Kathy is the window on the hill originally described by the Marraccinos. "I kept hearing about it. Then one evening I had to deliver a telephone message to the beach. As I walked back, I looked up and saw this great cathedral-like window on the side of the hill. It was very clear and I could see someone walking back and forth behind it.

"Something seemed to draw me toward the window, yet at the same time I felt that if I went there I'd never come back. I forced myself to return to the house. The next day I tramped all over the hill looking for some sign of what it might be, but found nothing. I never saw it again."

A few weeks later I returned to the house accompanied by a research team that included a group of mediums . The psychics walked about the house and grounds noting their impressions. I was the only one in the party who knew anything of the background of the place and I had not discussed it with anyone.

Chuck Pelton was the first of the mediums to speak. "There's a lot of current in the house, a lot of energy. Lights go on and off here by themselves."

"That's for sure!" Edwards affirmed. "The campers are always asking about those blinking lights. They say, 'Don't you and Kathy ever go to bed?' Actually the lights go on by themselves long after we've turned everything off and gone to sleep."

Chuck continued, "I see an old man wearing a raincoat and hat. I feel dampness, rain, mist. I think he was a sea captain."

This, of course, was corroborated by Kathy, who added that she'd found an old rain slicker and cap hanging on a hook on the back porch when they'd moved into the house. "At least a dozen people a year tell me they've seen an old man in a raincoat. I wonder sometimes if it couldn't be the sea captain who built this house in 1857."

The talking stopped. We were aware of the sound of animals howling outside. It was dark now and nothing could be seen from the windows. Chuck Pelton and Nick Nocerino went outside to investigate.

Sylvia Browne, director of the Nirvana Foundation, began to speak, "You feel a heaviness in your chest at night, don't you, Ralph?"

"Yes," he nodded.

She continued. "Things move around in this house. They seem to get lost, disappear for no apparent reason."

"They sure do," Kathy agreed. "The first year we lived here we were ready for the divorce court. I thought he'd taken things; he thought I had. Now I know that neither of us had. It was someone else, some*thing* else. Once I had a letter to deliver for one of the campers. It disappeared right out of my hand and appeared a day later in a laundry bag."

"I see an older man," Sylvia said. "He's wearing a long coat and walks about the grounds. In his life he killed an intruder. He doesn't like company even now. The people who lived here before were an angry, unhappy family. There was a lot of hatred, a lot of unresolved problems. I see unhappy young people ... a beautiful girl ... blood. There was a stabbing here. A baby died here, too. There were evil acts committed in the past."

Central Coast

Nick and Chuck had returned and I was very glad to see them. The atmosphere of the house had grown heavy and oppressive. I had a sense of danger, an emotion that I'd rarely experienced in the other houses investigated over the years. A dog was whining softly, cowering under a chair.

Nick Nocerino, a lifelong medium, sat down beside me. His words were anything but comforting. "There has been evil in this house—murder and incest. I see an angry man who dominated his children. They were virtual prisoners here."

Kathy recalled that the former owner, a woman in her nineties, was the last of a large family who had lived for decades in the isolated farmhouse. "The stories she told me of her life were sad," Kathy said. "Her father took all the children out of school and refused to allow their friends to visit. He forced his children to work long hours in his dairy and then, as his health failed, he made them wait on him hand and foot. She seemed very bitter."

Nick went on, "There's been smuggling here—people mostly. People were brought here and some of them never left. They're buried here. There was bootlegging too."

"Yes," Edwards agreed, "we found bottles of homemade whiskey and the remains of a still."

"A young girl came to visit about the turn of the century. Her name was Gwendolyn. She was murdered."

Kathy gasped... "A girl named Gwendolyn *did* disappear mysteriously while visiting her uncle, who owned the place. That was in the very early 1900s. No one ever heard from her again. But a couple of years ago Ralph and I decided to put in a barbecue pit and dug up a skeleton. Thinking that we might have tapped into an old Indian burial ground, we called in an expert from UC Santa Cruz. He said the bones were those of a woman buried eighty to ninety years ago."

The number of amazing "hits" says a good deal for mediumship, but did little to allay my fears. Directly across from where I sat in the living room was a window facing onto the front yard. From time to time I saw streaks and blobs of light at the window. It's my imagination, I told myself.

I could live with that until Ethel Pelton who was sitting on the floor opposite me and directly under the window, spoke in a tight, choked voice. "I feel something terrible behind me. Something's going on outside. I know it is and I'm scared."

It really didn't help to have my skeptical friend, John Wilson, a Menlo Park attorney, confide that he too felt a sense of dread and oppression.

It was nearly midnight as the seance broke up. John and I walked out into the black night. A thick fog was creeping in from the sea. I felt certain that the evil presence menacing the Edwards house had attached itself to me. Sick with terror, I stood shivering in the damp sea air—uncertain whether to continue on in the dark or go back into the afflicted house.

John made the decision for me. "Come on, let's get out of this place," he said, grasping my arm and pulling me toward the car. Just as we got in a great dark bird appeared out of nowhere and hovered above us. As we slowly navigated the narrow dirt road to the highway, the ugly creature preceded us. It had a wingspan of some six feet. What was it, I wondered—an owl, an eagle? I recalled the place had at one time been known as the Eagle Run Dairy. What a relief when this gruesome harbinger of doom finally faded away in the night.

But that was not the end of our troubles. A heavy wind seemed to come up out of nowhere as we crossed the Santa Cruz mountains, making it difficult to keep the car on the road. I began to see flashes of light like bolts of lightning and blobs of white energy. There seemed no doubt that some evil presence was pursuing us.

Central Coast

Some of that apprehension dissipated in the familiar atmosphere of my apartment. The streaks were gone, the blobs were gone, yet I could not rid myself of the feeling that I wasn't alone. Many times

Spirit photograph by Nocerino/Pelton team.

in the days that followed, I glanced up from my typewriter, certain that someone was looking over my shoulder.

Had I picked up a spectral hitchhiker? I recalled the story of "Lu," a woman who had visited the farmhouse with her boyfriend, a long time friend of the Edwardses. Lu had felt so uncomfortable in the house that she'd left almost immediately. At home, she experienced a sense of possession. Again and again she heard the words, *unfinished* and *unburied*. She saw a vision of a man and large searing white spots.

Slowly as the days passed, the sense of being watched diminished. I was alone again — really alone — and very glad of it. It was all imagination, I decided, and was beginning to believe it. And then one evening Nick called.

It seemed that he and Chuck had photographed the house while outdoors investigating the howling sounds. "What did you get, werewolves?" I tried to sound flippant.

"No, just blobs and streaks of light," he answered, also trying to sound flippant.

The pictures had been taken in darkness and yet the house was clearly revealed. The upstairs window of a darkened bedroom was illuminated and above the living room — where the seance had taken place — were round blobs of light and sometimes lightning-like bolts.

Some nights I wonder what they're doing down at the nude beach—but so far, I haven't had nerve enough to go back and find out.

The Red, White and Blue Beach is located on Highway 1 six miles north of Santa Cruz — look for the red, white and blue mailbox on the seaside of the road.

MOSS BEACH DISTILLERY

WHO IS THE MYSTERIOUS "BLUE LADY" WHO RETURNS TO haunt the cliffside restaurant, her high heels echoing a phantom Charleston eerily into the night?

Moss Beach Distillery past & present street view.

Some whisper that she's the unfortunate Virginia Rappe who died during a party hosted by Roscoe "Fatty" Arbuckle, the legendary silent film star, in his St. Francis Hotel suite.

Calling the affair an "unhallowed orgy," the unscrupulous district attorney saw to it that Arbuckle was tried and condemned in the press, then prosecuted him not one time but three in one of the most sensational cases in San Francisco history.

Virginia was described as a model, a starlet and a few other things. The murder weapon was said to have been a coke bottle. Others speculated that Arbuckle crushed her with his own weight. The first two trials resulted in a hung jury, the third gained Arbuckle an outright acquittal. It was a hollow victory. His career ruined, the former comedian died a broken man a few years later.

But what about Virginia? Many believe the pretty party girl returns in spirit to the speakeasy built on the site of another ill-fated watering hole that burned down a few years before.

The Moss Beach Distillery, originally a hotel-cum-whorehouse built in 1919, was constructed on a steep cliff overlooking the sea during an era when the Half Moon Bay area was notorious as San Francisco's biggest supplier of illegal liquor from Canada. The abundance of secluded beaches and coves along the isolated stretch of rugged ocean was an open invitation to rum runners. Bootlegging was dangerous business, murder and hijacking common. But that didn't stop film stars and politicians from flocking there. Virginia Rappe was remembered as being one of the liveliest. It's easy to imagine her drawn to the scene of earlier revelries, mischievously startling staff and patrons for more than seventy years.

Moss Beach Distillery front ocean view. Photograph by Deborah Wilson

Others suggest a Dashiell Hammett heroine as the legend's source. His girl with silver eyes wore a glistening blue gown and frequented a coastal roadhouse. Surely something or someone delights in opening and closing the creaky ladies room door and dancing a lively Charleston in seemingly empty rooms.

In 1990 when the present owner, John Barber, acquired the property his attempt to take inventory was blocked—literally. The wine cellar, a windowless room, was built into the side of a hill. Though unlocked, it took three men to force open the one door. When they finally succeeded, they realized that they'd been pushing against the entire wine supply. Who or what had shoved those boxes into position? How did that person exit the blocked doorway? The blue lady must have a lot of muscle!

Central Coast

It was around this time that Barber began having troubles with his brand new computer. Just out of the crate, it was somehow backdated to 1926.

Servers closing out late at night were plagued not only by a ringing pay phone but a buzzing house intercom. No one waited on the other end—no one human, anyway.

Then Jan Mucklestone, an artist who was helping Barber with the restaurant, began to have a sense that someone was watching her in the seemingly empty restroom. "It got so scary, I was afraid to use it," she recalls today. At this point she decided to call in a medium.

A séance was conducted by psychic Sylvia Browne at the request of NBC TV's *Unsolved Mysteries*. Almost immediately Browne picked up on a presence in the restroom. "It's a man. I get the name John Cantina. He was a bad guy, a rum runner. Oh! It was an awful death. He was castrated."

During the course of the evening, Browne made contact with a melancholy shade who identified herself as Mary Ellen Moreley. It seemed that Mary Ellen had died nearby in an automobile accident. Her last thoughts were of her three-year-old son. She lamented leaving him motherless and now—unaware of the passage of time—comes back to hunt for him him.

Mucklestone did some sleuthing in the records of the San Mateo Times. In 1920 the body of a man washed ashore near the Moss Beach Distillery. He had been castrated. Was he John Cantina?

Also the newspaper search revealed the death of a Mary Ellen Moreley, the victim of a car crash, which occurred close to the area. As a result of exposure on the TV show, Moreley's son, now a man in his 80s living in Florida, contacted the Moss Beach Distillery. His daughter—Mary Ellen's granddaughter—came to visit.

Yet many insist the ghost is yet another habitue of the speakeasy. This candidate loved two things; the color blue and the piano player. The second love proved her undoing for the pianist was the jealous sort who didn't take kindly to her flirtations with the clientele. One night he stabbed her to death in a jealous rage on the beach below the restaurant.

Over the years chefs, waitresses and patrons have not only heard the ghost, but seen her. Managers working late at night would hear all the faucets suddenly come on. They'd go to shut them off and return to find their office locked from the inside. Once a young boy ran screaming from the restroom where he'd been confronted by a woman in blue — covered with blood. Another night an out of towner stopped at the restaurant and asked the bartender, "Who was murdered here? I feel very strong vibrations over there," she explained, pointing to the spot where the piano once stood.

An even stranger tale was reported by Sheriff's Deputy Jim Belding who attended an impromptu seance with several employees at the restaurant. There was an inexplicable cold spot and a candle that suddenly ignited—but no apparition.

Belding and his partner left the restaurant at 3:30 a. m. and headed north on Highway 92. Then suddenly Belding's car developed a mind of its own — swerving first to the right and then to the left. A blazing white light appeared before them. Belding swerved once again, smashing the car. Miraculously they survived the crash and went off in search of help. When they returned a tow truck was already on the scene.

Later, when Belding went to pick up his car, the tow truck driver inquired about "the lady." When Belding looked blank, the mechanic persisted, "The pretty girl in the short blue dress, kind of like a costume. She was standing in the road crying and bleeding."

The deputy just shook his head.

The Moss Beach Distillery is located on the corner of Beach and Ocean streets in Moss Beach. Telephone: (415) 728-5595.

Central Coast

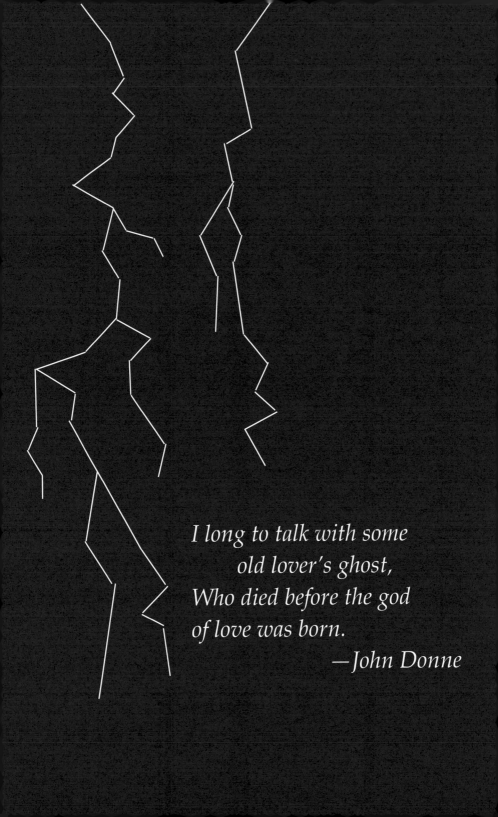

I long to talk with some
    old lover's ghost,
Who died before the god
of love was born.
                    —John Donne

LOS ANGELES AREA

THE REAL GHOST BUSTERS

THELMA TODD'S GARAGE

HERITAGE PARK

THE ELKE SOMMER-JOE HYAMS HOUSE

THE QUEEN MARY

THE REAL
GHOSTS BUSTERS

BARRY TAFF AND KERRY GAYNOR WOULD LIKE TO SHED some new light on an old subject—how to catch a ghost.

So far the way has not been easy. Once Barry's fountain pen was stolen by a ghost. Another time he was nearly strangled to death by a possessed subject. Once eight people watched in horror as a fifteen pound flower pot was suddenly levitated to the ceiling and then dumped—with force enough to kill—directly between the two researchers.

But far more shocking was the fate of their prize subject, "Mrs. B" of Culver City, who says she was raped by three spirits. Not too surprisingly, the B family had reached the point of desperation when the psychic research teamed was called in from the Neuropsychiatric Institute on the UCLA campus. The group was headed by Barry Taff, a parapsychologist with a Ph.D. in psychophysiology, and Kerry Gaynor, a UCLA graduate student.

Mrs. B, a divorcee in her mid-thirties, lived in a dilapidated house which had twice been condemned by the city. Her family consisted of herself, a six year old daughter and three sons, ages ten, thirteen and sixteen. All described a particular apparition they called "Mr. Whose-it." which appeared to them in solid form and was just over six feet tall. Mrs. B and her eldest son had also seen two other entities, solid figures with oriental faces who appeared in Mrs. B's bedroom.

The B family emphatically dismissed the theory that the figures might have been imagined—they were far too vivid for that. Mrs. B told of being sexually assaulted by the three beings on several occasions and had the bruises to prove it.

During their ten week investigation of the house, the research team was frequently aware of intense cold spots and the strong, sometimes overpowering smell of decomposing flesh in Mrs. B's bedroom. Both the stench and cold spots faded in and out at random, sometimes disappearing completely. A thorough examination of the house offered no explanation.

One evening while Kerry was talking to the older son in the kitchen, a lower cabinet suddenly swung open and a pan flew out following a curved path before crashing to the floor nearly three feet from the cabinet.

On more than twenty occasions during the investigations, the team— which sometimes numbered as many as twenty researchers — witnessed a spectral light show which had an expanding, contracting appearance sometimes encompassing Mrs. B's entire bedroom.

In order to rule out the possibility of outside influences, such as reflections from street lights, or passing cars,—causing the lights, heavy quilts and bedspreads were placed against the windows. This seemed to have no effect upon the show which now appeared even more brilliantly against the darkened surroundings.

Mrs. B's son told the team that his Black Sabbath and Uriah Heep records seemed to infuriate the spirit. Reactions appeared particularly strong when the themes dealt with devil worship. As an experiment, the records were played in the presence of the group. Light activity dramatically increased, reaching a crescendo that appeared to match the feverish pitch of the music.

One evening it became apparent to the twenty researchers present that the lights were responding to provocative remarks made by Mrs. B. "In fact," Taff says, "when Mrs. B began to swear at the lights, assuming that they were in some manner related to the entities that attacked her, the lights intensified beyond all previous displays. It almost seemed as if the lights were the direct product

Los Angeles Area

of Mrs. B's psychic state, peaking and dipping in accordance with her emotional fluctuations."

One of the most interesting events of the evening involved the use of a geiger counter. As the lights reacted to peak intensity, the registration of background radiation—previously constant—suddenly dropped to zero.

When the light activity began to dwindle, fade and finally stop, the geiger counter's meter returned to its normal level of background radiation.

At the next session the lights began to take shape, forming the partial three dimensional image of a man whose shoulders, head and arms were readily discernible by each of the twenty individuals present.

Despite the battery of cameras clicking steadily away during these sessions, almost nothing of the light show was picked up on film. Yet another night when nothing was happening lightwise, Taff photographed a small ball of light that no one had seen.

"I took the picture on an impulse," he explains. "A sudden rush of cold current and a pervasive stench seemed to flow from the closed bedroom door. I shot the picture in the hall, seemingly of a wall and a closed door. Though none of us saw anything, the camera recorded a ball of light about a foot in diameter."

During the three month period of investigation the phenomena seemed to intensify. Mrs. B told of being chased by a pair of candelabra which took off from the kitchen sink and flew across the room—a distance of some twelve feet—and struck her arm. The group examined her large bruise.

Mrs. B's twelve year old son, who witnessed the event, said that the flying candelabra barely missed him. The B's also told Taff that a large wooden board which had been nailed to the wall beneath one of the bedroom windows was torn loose from its secured position as if by unseen hands and propelled some fifteen feet across the room, narrowly missing the boy's head before falling harmlessly to the floor.

In an effort to escape the phenomena, the B family moved to a new home. For a time this appeared to pacify the forces which seemed to delight in persecuting them—but not for long. They were besieged again. Who was it?

Taff and Gaynor believe the evidence gives every indication of a discarnate intelligence and have recommended an exorcism.

* * *

Taff and Gaynor became involved in another equally bizarre case when two men employed in the UCLA photo lab told them of a party they'd attended where "books just flew around by themselves."

Not your typical Hollywood party, they agreed and went on to check out the house. What they found was a charming Spanish Colonial, vintage 1921, with a romantic past—Barbara Stanwyck and Robert Taylor once lived there. The owner, Don Jolly, a senior vice president of a savings and loan company, admitted that strange things did happen about the place. Only the week before his houseboy had quit, complaining that cabbages chased him about the house.

* * *

Taff and Gaynor then returned to Jolly's house with a KTTV news team. Almost immediately an ice tray flew from the kitchen and crossed the living room where it crashed against a far wall. Next a large shower head from an upstairs bathroom floated through the living room where it finally fell to the floor in full view of fifteen people.

While standing in the bar area, Don Jolly and Taff were pelted by a shower of coins which appeared to fall from the empty air.

Los Angeles Area

Don Jolly's house. Photograph by C.J. Marrow

Coasters took off from the dining room table soaring into the living room and a large sack of napkins flew out of the kitchen into the dining room followed by a large, heavy pewter goblet which struck the wall with enough force to rip off the plaster.

The outside of the house proved equally hazardous. Richard Matheson, Jr., a member of the news team, was nearly struck on the head by a flying shoe as he searched the grounds.

Newscaster Connie Fox, hoping to escape the flying objects inside, ran out onto the front porch only to be chased by a World Book Atlas that intercepted her on the walkway and chased her down the front stairs. (In order to accomplish this, the Atlas had to make three distinct turns, as the walkway of the hillside home is constructed in a Z-shape.) Members of the team who witnessed the event said that the pursuing book was almost birdlike as it flapped its pages.

Barry noted that the electricity within the house seemed to turn itself on and off at will throughout the evening, selectively negating specific circuits. Whenever the KTTV crew attempted to film the house, their power was cut off while other circuits were unaffected. Even battery powered equipment such as tape recorders and electronic camera flashes refused to function. The street lamp directly in front of Jolly's house was effected, though the other street lights on the block continued to glow.

No one was too surprised when Don Jolly sold the house just three months later.

Trafton House   Photograph by C.J. Marrow

* * *

The most mysterious case ever investigated by the team was the Trafton home in Pacific Palisades.   It began when Bliss Trafton, a young school teacher, approached Taff one evening at UCLA. "You're going to think I'm crazy when I tell you this, but there's a ghost dressed in armor who walks around our house at night." She then went on to describe the symptoms, almost ordinary —to Taff —cold spots and objects that moved from room to room of their own volition.

Taff went to investigate the house and almost immediately lost a prize pen. "It was a rather expensive pen," he says, "distinguished by a bent clip and sliver ornamentation—it couldn't be mistaken for another. I'd hardly set it down on the coffee table in front of me before it disappeared. I'd only been in the room a few seconds, my pen and notebook sitting there before me. Then when I went to pick up my pen, it was gone.

"Of course we looked under the furniture thinking that it might have rolled off—but it hadn't. No one had left the room, no one had picked it up without my noticing. The pen simply wasn't there. Finally we just gave up and went on with the investigation. A few minutes later I found my pen in a rear bedroom of the house. How do you explain that one?"

During the visit, Barry and his team experienced the same cold spots and pounding noises that the Trafton family had reported.

A surprising postscript occurred a few months later when the Traftons decided to add on to the rear of their home. While digging the foundation, workmen uncovered graves containing skeletons dressed in armor of the type worn by the Spanish conquistadors.

* * *

Barry Taff considers his most fascinating haunting to have occurred in Inglewood. It's the only case where he has personally encountered direct malevolent activity. The manifestations began, he says, with apparitions of deceased prior occupants. Many of the neighbors who didn't know that the former owners were dead continued to see them at their daily chores about the house and grounds.

On several occasions individuals inside the house saw a variety of objects being flung about or floating through the air. Doors and windows opened and closed of their own accord and the sounds of a man walking about the house were heard. They also noticed that a display case remained dust free as if it were being polished daily while other pieces of furniture in the unoccupied house were heavily laden with dust.

"The results of a seance conducted in the house were startling to everyone—but nearly fatal to me," Taff said. "As some twenty people watched, one of the sitters—the grandson of a deceased prior occupant of the house—became violent and suddenly attacked me. He seemed to snarl as his fingers tightened about my throat. The man's actions were like one possessed. 'Get out of my house! This is *my* house!' It took five large men to drag him off me—they had to knock him unconscious to do it. When the man came to, he had no recollection of what had happened. His last memory was of *someone* saying 'Get out of my house.'

"During the attack by the twenty five year old man, the others present didn't see *him* attack me. Instead they saw an older, larger, white haired man.

"The attack broke up the evening. The next day I received a call from a neighbor. He claimed to have seen the old man out in the yard and had heard the sounds of something being smashed inside the house.

"Upon our return the next evening, we observed that all the furniture with the exception of the well-dusted display case had been thrown to the floor. The house was littered with broken glass and almost every drawer had been pulled out and its contents strewn about the floor.

"It should be noted that the grandson who had attacked me elected to subject himself to intensive psychological testing in order to determine whether he had a latent capacity for unprovoked violence of this degree. His psychiatric and psychological profile indicated that there was no such tendency.

"I could only conclude from this that his mind and body had somehow been seized by the grandfather, who for his own reasons, resented my presence in the house."

* * *

"What does it all mean?" Taff asks today. "We began our investigations hoping to explain ghosts or explain them away. Twenty years later, we can do neither. My search remains where it began. I can only explain haunting as I did at the beginning: a *phenomenon*.

Maybe the next house. ..."

Los Angeles Area

THELMA TODD'S GARAGE

THE LAST THING THAT DISTRICT ATTORNEY BURON FITTS wanted was another Hollywood scandal. In the 1920s and 30s Los Angeles was totally dependent upon the movie industry for its survival—one more scandal could turn a fickle public off completely. But there was another more personal reason. His own reputation was badly tarnished from a series of inept criminal investigations. Another claim of mismanagement could sink him for good.

Perhaps that's why the murder of glamorous and infamous Thelma Todd was never solved.

Dubbed as "the Hot Toddy," "the Ice Cream Blonde" and "the Blonde Venus," Thelma was gorgeous—so gorgeous that a jaded film mogul offered her a movie job on the strength of one photograph alone. Following her 1926 introduction in *Fascinating Youth,* Thelma made 107 films in the next nine years.

By 1935 she was 29, queen of the silver screen and starring with such luminaries as Gary Cooper, Humphrey Bogart, Laurel and Hardy, the Marx Brothers, Buster Keaton, Joe E. Brown and Zazu Pitts.

And Thelma was bright as well as beautiful. Aware that the glitz couldn't last forever, she invested in an elegant Palisades roadhouse with part time lover, Roland West.

Todd and West shared adjoining apartments above the restaurant and parked their cars in a large garage, topped by a loft, far above and behind the cafe on a cliff. This was attached to a mansion owned by Carmen Jewel, West's estranged wife.

Within weeks the restaurant was a favorite of the rich and famous of the day. Everyone liked Thelma. Besides looks, brains, talent and the sizzling "hot toddy" reputation — she was *nice*, bubbly, fun to be with. It would appear that this was a woman who had everything.

Then on Monday morning, December 16, 1935, Thelma's maid opened the garage door and found the actress slumped behind the wheel of her car, her eyes closed.

Thelma Tood — the blond Venus in a 1928 publicity still.

She was wearing a full-length mink coat over a metallic blue sequined evening gown and matching cape, blue silk slippers and about $20,000 worth of jewelry. It was, in fact, the exact same outfit that the maid had dressed Thelma in to attend a celebrity studded gala the previous Saturday night.

"What a party!" the maid thought and walked around to the driver's side, thinking she could waken the sleeping star. But Thelma was not sleeping it off—she was dead.

That such a thing could be seemed incredible, but what happened next was even more incredible. Despite the fact that there was blood on Thelma's head and face, her dress, her coat, the car and the garage floor, and that two ribs, her nose and a tooth were broken, the official police version was that the actress had died by her own hand, perhaps intentionally.

District Attorney Buron Fitts's story was that Thelma Todd, finding herself locked out of her apartment, had climbed the 271 steps from the street to the garage and had huddled for warmth in the front seat of her Lincoln, then started the engine, and been asphyxiated by exhaust fumes. The death, he insisted—despite bodily evidence to the contrary—had taken place early Sunday morning.

Alice Todd, Thelma's mother—a screen mother straight from central casting—was a strong, aggressive woman who knew her mind and never hesitated to speak it. Now she confronted the district attorney head on: "You know my daughter was murdered. I know my daughter was murdered. You also know that I know a lot of people in town. Big people. Important people. There's going to be an investigation. Either you solve this, Mr. Fitts, or I'll do a little investigating of my own."

The door had hardly slammed shut before reports began to come in from a variety of credible witnesses who had seen the actress on Sunday —when the police report had placed Thelma dead in her car.

The possibilities were endless. The beautiful Thelma Todd might have had any man but instead was drawn to a list of highly unsavory characters. Many might think the reasons were psychological. The daughter of a crooked politician, Thelma learned about the underworld literally on her father's knee. Among her earliest memories were the power plays of police, politicians and gangsters who had partied in her own home.

Was she seeking the love of a father who had been too busy for her when she became involved with a series of cruel and violent men?

Thelma's one and only marriage was to Pasquale "Pat" DiCicco, a wealthy playboy with a nasty streak and Mafia connections. At first Pat was madly in love with Thelma, whom he called, "my Lambie." The couple eloped in 1932 but divorced within two years.

DiCicco had reappeared in Thelma's life shortly before her death. There were rumors that he wanted her back and sought an active involvement in her restaurant. She rebuffed him.

DiCicco then wangled an invitation from Stanley Lupino and his daughter, Ida, who had hosted the Saturday night affair at Sunset Strip's trendy Trocadero in Thelma's honor. Though the special guest attended the party alone, DiCicco appeared with actress Margaret Lindsay on his arm. Some said there'd been angry words between the formerly marrieds.

Later Thelma's friends walked with her to the chauffeur-driven limousine rented for the evening. Before getting in Thelma turned to her entourage with a grand flourish and called out "good-bye." It was a gesture none of them would ever forget.

All the way back to her apartment Thelma, professing fear of kidnap or murder, urged the driver, Ernest Peters, to go faster. They were being followed, he would later say, by gangsters. They reached the roadhouse at 3:45 a. m. Though Peters ordinarily walked Thelma to the front door, surprisingly she now refused his offer. Despite her earlier fears, she dismissed the chauffeur. "That won't be necessary. Go home, Ernest." As Peters drove off, Thelma approached the darkened building alone.

The actions of Roland West, Thelma's partner and on-again-off-again lover, were also strange. Sid Grauman had called him at the restaurant at about 2:30 to say that Thelma would be leaving soon and would be home in about an hour. West later testified that he'd bolted the heavy door locking her out and then went to bed. Just why he did this, no one asked; and West never told.

But there were neighbors who testified to hearing an angry exchange between West and Thelma, that he'd literally shoved her out the door and that she'd beat on it calling to him for ten minutes to let her in.

Los Angeles Area

Neither the police nor the grand jury pressed the matter, though Thelma's friends pointed out that West had directed such mystery thrillers as *Alibi, The Monster* and *The Bat Whispers.* The ex-director, they said, had an affinity for convoluted murder mysteries and a fascination with "the perfect crime."

But there was yet another suspect, a man so evil that his very name was synonymous with the devil. The man was Charles "Lucky" Luciano, but behind his back, they called him "Charley Lucifer." The most feared and hated of all the underworld bosses, he had no friends, only those who were afraid not to go along with him. One of these was Pat DiCicco.

It was Pat who introduced Luciano to his then wife; and, for a time it was thought that Thelma and the gangster were lovers. It is known that Luciano introduced her to drugs. Very probably he wanted her total dependence on him. But Thelma was strong. After a time she began to pull away from Luciano and his sinister influence—something nobody did. When the gangster announced that he wanted gambling on the third floor of her roadhouse, the actress rebelled. "You'll open a gambling casino in my restaurant over my dead body!" she told him.

"That can be arranged," he coolly reminded her.

So here was the cast of characters: a jealous lover, a vindictive and violent ex-husband with connections to the most hated and feared mobster in this country or any other; and, finally, the mobster himself—Charley Lucifer.

Then quite suddenly Alice Todd stopped her pressure on the police. Now she was claiming that her daughter's death *was* accidental. Many thought she seemed frightened. "Several witnesses have not told all they know," said one juror. A cover-up was suspected. "Some of those who appear most mute, most dumb, apparently are deliberately concealing facts," complained George Rochester, grand-jury foreman. "Potent Hollywood interests have attempted to block the probe (into Todd's death) from the beginning."

Whoever was doing what—it worked. The witnesses stuck to their stories. The questions that might have triggered revealing testimony were never asked. In the end, the grand jury brought the investigation to a close. Thelma Todd's death was ruled an accident. Case closed, but not solved.

*   *   *

Roland West, always considered a prime suspect, never made another movie. Shortly after Thelma's death., he and his estranged wife, Carmen Jewell, were divorced. Soon he sold the cafe and went into seclusion. There was a stroke, a nervous breakdown. In 1951 on his deathbed, West confessed to Thelma's murder. Delirious at the time, he spoke again and again of locking his lover out—most certainly a contributing factor to her eventual death. Had she been safe inside, Thelma would certainly not have had a rendezvous with the real killer.

West had another reason to feel guilty and had often spoken of it. It was he who had caved in to the pressure from Luciano's men who had infiltrated the restaurant, placing Thelma on a collision course with Luciano.

Was West guilty? Most certainly. Of murder? It seems unlikely.

Charles "Lucky" Luciano never returned to Los Angeles after the murder. He was eventually squeezed out of his West Coast holdings by Chicago mobsters and considered the area the one place unlucky for him. It was the beginning of his fall from power.

Finally deported to his hometown in Sicily as an undesirable alien, he was never questioned or called to testify in the murder of Thelma Todd, though his name was mentioned by everyone who knew her. Luciano himself was above the law—and certainly strong enough to prevent the questioning of his underling, Pat DiCicco, as well.

Los Angeles Area

One of the strangest stories regarding the murder involves a black and gold sardonyx ring which Pat DiCicco gave to Thelma shortly after their marriage. Inside the band was the inscription, "To Lambie." Thelma continued to wear the ring after their divorce. Though more than $20,000 in jewels were found on the victim, the ring was reported missing.

Then in 1979 while touring in Warren, Ohio in the musical *Irene*, Patsy Kelley — an old friend of Thelma's — was approached backstage by a mysterious man. "This was Miss Todd's," he said, handing her the ring; then turned without another word and left.

And then there's another odd twist, a strangely prophetic one. In the movie *Monkey Business*, co-starring Thelma and Groucho Marx, the latter uttered the enigmatic line: *"I know, I know. You're a woman who's been getting nothing but bad breaks, but you'll have to stay in the garage all night."* Now what did that mean?

A strange, sad, mystifying story; but is it over?

The sidewalk cafe is now owned by Paulist Productions. Thelma and Roland's apartments are now one work area. The downstairs cafe is a storage room.   The third floor—which Luciano wanted for gambling—is an apartment. The main entrance still has the two wooden doors, each with a glass diamond-shaped panel etched with the word "joyas," just as in Thelma's day.

Many who work in the building insist they've seen the ghost of Thelma Todd passing through the hall at the top of the staircase near the outside doors to the courtyard moving through her old apartment. Psychics have been overcome by noxious fumes in the garage where Todd's body was found and others have heard the sound of a car engine running when they knew the garage was empty.

Thelma Todd's Sidewalk Cafe was at 17575 Pacific Coast Highway at the corner of Porto Marina in Pacific Palisades. The structure is well preserved. The garage is up the hill at 17531 Posetano Road.

HERITAGE PARK

NOT ONLY IS HERITAGE PARK HAUNTED, BUT POSSIBLY former caretaker, Don Hayes, is as well.

One night, Don says, he was lying in bed wide awake when an apparition of a man appeared before him. "You know who I am," the spectre said by way of introduction, then advised: "Don't take any bullshit."

"Unfortunately, I *don't* know who he is," Don admitted, "but I do think a lot about his message."

Another strange incident occurred one evening when Don was rehearsing a play with the Scheherazade Players in an old barn at the rear of the park which had been converted into a theater. The seating capacity of the place is limited, the ambience intimate. "The audience is very close to the stage and we can see each individual quite clearly," Don explains. "While going over my lines, I noticed an older man sitting in the front row. I assumed that he must be the father of a cast member but wondered why he was dressed in such old fashioned looking clothes. As soon as the scene was over, I started toward him to introduce myself—only to see him disappear before my eyes."

The Scheherazade Players—or possibly their barn—may have been responsible for still a different type of phenomena. While the group was performing *The Valkyrie*, a friend took a series of pictures. When the roll was developed, they found what looks like bolts of white lightning superimposed over the original subjects. Many parapsychologists believe this type of phenomenon indicates the presence of spirits or spirit energy.

A highlight of the two acre Heritage Park is the Stanley House which was built in 1891 and has been retained in all its ginger-

Los Angeles Area

bread elegance. Inside, two pictures continue to mystify a steady stream of tourists who come to view the old house which has been turned into a museum. First, there's the portrait of J. G. Chandler, whose serious face can occasionally break into an unexpected smile. Then, there's the more sinister visage of an unidentified man who appears to bleed at the throat. Studying the latter portrait carefully, one sees what appears to be tiny beads of blood forming just above the starched white collar spreading to a dark red line along the throat.

Spirit energy at Heritage Park.

Recently a team from Psychic Science Investigators visited the house. Several felt, while climbing the stairs to the second floor, that their progress was impeded. Later, learning the background of the house, they discussed the former owner, Agnes Ware Stanley, and speculated as to whether they were not reliving a fragment of the pain and frustration which she must have felt as the years passed and she was no longer able to climb the stairs. In the later years of Mrs. Stanley's long life the second floor was closed off entirely.

Many visitors to the home have been puzzled by an unexpected noise, the sound of a baby crying in the upstairs nursery. Members of the PSI team heard it too. While resting their hands on the crib, some received impressions of an infant's death. It was later learned that Jennifer Null, the baby daughter of the former caretaker, had died in the room.

Heritage Park is located at 12174 Euclid Avenue in Garden Grove.

THE ELKE SOMMER— JOE HYAMS HOUSE

It began prosaically enough with afternoon tea. Elke Sommer invited Edith Dahlfeld, a German journalist, to have tea with her by the pool of her Beverly Hills home. It was July 6, 1964.

Glancing up from the tea table, Mrs. Dahlfeld saw a man come from the dining area of the house and walk toward them. Wondering idly why they had not been introduced, she watched as he strode briskly around the pool. Mrs. Dahlfeld was to describe him later as a middle aged gentleman dressed formally in a black suit, white shirt and tie. His hair was thinning at the top, she said, and he had a bulbous "potato" nose.

Mrs. Dahlfeld's attention was diverted by the general conversation and she turned away from the solitary figure. Glancing back a few seconds later she was surprised to see that he was gone. "What happened to that man?" she asked.

Elke shook her head in bewilderment. "What man?" She had seen nothing. *There were no other guests.*

From then on screen star Elke Sommer and her writer husband, Joe Hyams, began to hear the sounds of chairs being pushed back in the dining room as though guests were rising from some ghostly dinner party. After a few nights of this, Hyams cut away all the branches which had been rubbing against the dining room window. The sounds did not stop.

In August Elke went to Yugoslavia to make a movie, leaving her husband alone in the house — or so they thought.

The noises in the dining room continued. On three occasions a locked window seemingly unlocked itself in the night and was

Los Angeles Area

wide open in the morning. Twice Hyams heard the front door open and shut even though it was found to be bolted in the morning.

Before joining his wife in Yugoslavia, Hyams arranged to have a detective check the house periodically in their absence. The man reported finding doors and windows wide open, although nothing was missing. Once, while driving by the house at two-thirty in the morning, he discovered all the lights on. Just as he pulled in the drive, they went off. An electrician checked the fuse box and lines but could find nothing wrong.

When the couple returned it was to the same restless dining room chairs. Now Elke's dogs began to react as though to a presence that no one else saw. "They would suddenly start to bark while staring toward the entrance of the dining room," Hyam recalls. "The puppy often ran to a certain spot in the dining room and then trotted out exactly as if following at someone's heels."

In August of 1965, the couple closed the house again and went on a month's vacation. During this time Marvin Chandler, the pool maintenance man, was surprised to catch a glimpse through the terrace windows of a man walking through the dining room. Chandler noted that the man's hands were clasped behind his back. He was a tall, heavy-set, elderly man wearing dark trousers, a tie and white shirt.

Having previously been told that the owners were away and the house empty, the maintenance man went inside to investigate. "He just seemed to evaporate before my eyes," Chandler recalls.

The apparition next appeared to John Sherlock, a writer who was staying alone in the house during the couple's absence. He reported seeing a man of about fifty dressed in dark slacks and a white shirt with a necktie but no jacket, standing in the family room which adjoins the dining room. "I have never had such a feeling of menace," Sherlock said later. "I couldn't get out fast enough." Although it was well past midnight, Sherlock dressed quickly and departed—spending the rest of the night in a motel.

The last witness was a real estate broker who was spending the night in the guest room. Once again the family was away and the witness was alone in the house. The apparition later described by the realtor was a middle aged man who seemed to be searching for something. The ghost was seen in both the living room and the guest room. On this occasion he was reported wearing dark slacks and a T-shirt.

Convinced that something thoroughly unpleasant was going on, the couple called in the American Society for Psychical Research. Dr. Thelma Moss, then a member of the Neuropsychiatric Institute, UCLA, organized a special group of investigators—mediums and researchers from the A.S.P.R.—to survey the house under controlled conditions.

Dr. Moss began by interviewing the witnesses. On the basis of their data, four measuring devices were devised. These included checklists of physical activities, descriptive adjectives, and qualities relating to the ghost, and a location chart of the house and grounds.

The witnesses were first asked to score the checklists. Then a number of psychics were invited to tour the house independently of one another. Afterward they were to indicate on the checklist their impressions of the ghost, his appearance and activities. Finally a control group of non-sensitives was asked to fill out the same forms *as if* they had seen a ghost in a house having such a floor plan.

The method, outlined by Dr. Moss in the October 1968 issue of the American Society of Psychical Research, began with the assignment of a draftsman to visit the house and make a rough sketch of the floor plan on its two levels, as well as a plan of the back garden and swimming pool area. The witnesses, the psychics and the non-psychic control group, were all asked to

Los Angeles Area

indicate on copies of the plan those areas where they felt the ghost had been seen or which they felt it had frequently occupied.

The "personality" of the ghost was defined by means of a checklist. Witnesses and subjects were asked to circle appropriate adjectives and to cross out adjectives opposite to the personality being described.

A list of forty active verbs was prepared describing various types of activities (music, pacing, helping, laughing, floating, crying, dancing, eating, attacking, singing, etc.) Witnesses and subjects were asked to circle those activities which most accurately described what the ghost seemed to be doing and to cross out activities opposite to what the ghost appeared to be doing.

To establish the personal appearance of the ghost, another list was compiled. Here the items which the witnesses had mentioned were disguised by use of a multiple choice technique with many false items.

The experimental group included eight psychics who had worked before with the Southern California branch of the A.S.P.R. The control group comprised eight members of the society who did not believe that they could sense the presence of the ghost. The latter agreed to perform the same tasks as the experimental group.

In order to avoid any contamination of information it was considered vital that the investigators who had interviewed the witnesses should not work with the eight psychics who comprised the experimental group and also that no investigator who knew one psychic's impressions would work with another psychic.

There were eight coworkers, one for each psychic. After driving the psychic to the house and being admitted by a servant, the coworker remained in the living room while the psychic wandered as she or he pleased through all the rooms of the house as well as around the garden and pool area.

Each psychic was given a plan of the house and grounds and asked to indicate on it those places where he felt the ghost had been—or might be at the time of the visit.

Once the psychics had completed their tours and filled out their descriptive forms, the eight volunteer subjects comprising the control group met at the office of the Psychical Society. They were then instructed to fill out the location charts and checklists *as if* they had been taken to a house reputed to be haunted by a male ghost. All the subjects complied and their data was used in the statistical analysis.

The similarities found among the reports of the psychics and the differences discovered among the control groups were startling. None of the guesses made by the control group were in agreement when their checklists were tabulated and only one of them achieved even marginal similarity with the account of a witness. By contrast, *the psychics were very similar in their perceptions.* A consistent pattern emerged among them that was statistically significant: a composite ghost who appeared to be over thirty-five, tall and of medium to heavy build.

Maxine Bell, after touring the house, returned to the dining room where she described a sloppy looking spectre in his fifties. "I think he's a doctor," she said. "He died of a heart attack and is determined to stay in the house."

The next day another psychic, Brenda Crenshaw, entered the dining room and said, "I see a man, above average height, about fifty-eight, a doctor who died of a chest or heart condition outside the country."

Joe Hyams was reminded of a doctor with whom he'd been writing a book who had died suddenly while the book was still in progress.

Hyams then questioned the previous owners of the house. "I never *saw* anything unusual," the woman said, thinking back over her

Los Angeles Area

eighteen month tenancy. "But I heard strange sounds frequently." She told of an evening when her husband was out of town. Awakened from a sound sleep by the sound of footsteps in the dining room, she telephoned a friend and asked if she might go to stay with her. Locking herself in the upstairs bedroom, she called a taxi. A short while later the cab arrived and stopped in the driveway by the front door.

"I waited for the driver to ring the bell, but he didn't. Finally I shouted to him from the bedroom window. When he answered I ran down the stairs and into the cab. When I asked why he hadn't rung the bell, he replied that he'd seen a man standing by the door and assumed that he was the fare. The man vanished when I called out."

The following year Elke Sommer and Joe Hyams attempted to rent their home for the summer while they traveled in Europe. Mrs. Red Buttons, when brought to the house by a realtor, refused to enter. "It has an evil aura," she said, adding that she'd never felt that way about a house before.

Finally Mr. and Mrs. Harry Kanter rented the house. To celebrate the uneventfulness of their three month sojourn, the Kanters gave a "Good-by Ghost Party." Sheet-clad guests had a pleasant —if uneventful time — until eleven-thirty when every light in the place went out. Suddenly a terrific crash was heard in the dining room. A wrought iron candelabra had crashed to the floor. It should be noted that there was no master switch to enable a practical joker to turn off all the lights simultaneously.

Elke Sommer and Joe Hyams moved back but the nocturnal activity within the house proved too much for them. They decided to move and began looking at houses. At last a selection was made. On March 12, 1967, the couple sat up late watching television—an old movie, *The Haunting.*

"I wonder what the ghost thinks about our moving," Hyams mused aloud. "If he has any opinion, he'd better express it pretty soon."

A few hours later Elke was awakened by the sound of pounding on their bedroom door.   As Hyams opened the door he heard muffled laughter. The hallway was filled with black smoke. The couple escaped by leaping from their second-story bedroom window.

Hyams thought ruefully of a prediction made by Jacqueline Eastlund a few months before. "I see your dining room in flames next year. Be careful." At the time he'd considered raising his insurance premium and regretted not doing so later.

Lotte von Strahl returned to the premises at Hyams' invitation. "The spirits have all been driven out by the fire," she aassured him. The house could be rebuilt, it would be safe now."

Elke and Joe considered. The ghostly knocking had saved them from being burned alive. Perhaps it was a warning: *get out.*

And that's exactly what they did.

Los Angeles Area

THE QUEEN MARY

IT BEGAN WITH A PROPHECY: *"THE QUEEN MARY, LAUNCHED today, will know her greatest fame and popularity when she never sails another mile and never carries another paying passenger."*

In 1936, as the fabulous ocean liner was prepared for its maiden voyage, Londoners thought the words of astrologer Lady Mabel Fortescue-Harrison very strange indeed.

The Queen's subsequent seagoing life was brilliant and varied. For thirty years she plied the seas, a floating haven for the rich and famous, an elegant backdrop for countless private dramas.

Then in 1966, the Queen dropped anchor for the last time.   And, as it turned out, the psychic noblewoman that everyone thought daft was absolutely right!   Today the ship is permanently berthed on Pier J in Long Beach — a 390-room hotel which also hosts tours, conventions and maritime exhibits every day of the year.

But that's really only the beginning of the story.   One of the Queen's greatest attractions is that many former crew members as well as passengers simply refuse to give up the ship.   The *Queen Mary* is haunted.

The strange occurrences began even before the ship was open to the public. In early 1966, the ocean liner was being readied at the Long Beach Shipyard for her new incarnation.   Each evening the work crew headed for home, leaving the great ship dark and silent except for security guards who patrolled the vessel, deck by deck accompanied by specially trained dogs.

It started one night as a guard approached the watertight door to Shaft Alley, a narrow passageway that provides access to the ship's propeller shafts. Suddenly his dog stopped and stared straight ahead, refusing to budge. Assuming that someone must be hiding nearby, the guard searched the area thoroughly but found nothing.

Returning to the dog, he attempted to push it through the door, but the animal simply would not move.

When the incident was reported, an investigation was conducted. It was learned that John Pedder, an 18-year-old crewman, had been crushed to death by that very doorway —number thirteen—during a routine watertight door drill.

Is he the "Shaft Alley spectre" who has since been reported

The Queen Mary

by so many? The description never varies: a young man with jet black hair and a beard wearing blue-gray overalls.

Once the Queen was open to the public, a series of unexplained events began. During a "sweep" of the ship at the end of the day, a tour guide was checking to make certain that no guests were left in the area. As she took the escalator, she saw a bearded man wearing overalls coming up behind her. Assuming that he was a lost guest, the guide waited for him to reach the top so that she could point out the exit. Turning at the landing above the escalator, she saw that the man had vanished.

But there's at least one other not so able bodied seaman aboard. A man wearing a white boiler room suit has been spotted in the same area. His uniform is that of the original crew members fifty years ago. Each sighting has found this devoted worker tinkering on some part of the ship's engines.

Los Angeles Area

On one occasion, two tour guides experienced yet another type of phenomenon. While standing on the Starting Platform of the Aft Engine Room, they heard a tinkling sound, and turned to see a chain dangling between two stanchions begin to jerk and sway as though an unseen hand was running along it, using the chain for support.

The kitchens of the *Queen Mary* are also said to have a guardian ghost. Cooks and busboys tell of strange visitations: strangers who enter and vanish, dishes moving by themselves, lights turning on or off, and utensils disappearing.

The Queen Mary's kitchen is also thought to be haunted.

The culprit, they believe, was a long ago cook. During the war, the *Queen Mary* was used as a troop ship. One night a tense and angry group of men became so incensed over the quality of the food they'd been served that they forced their way into the kitchen and started a riot. During the melee, a cook was thrown into a heated oven.

Equally bizarre are the tales of phantom "pool parties" in the swimming area. Security guards go to investigate the sounds of splashing and laughter only to find the large pool empty, the water still. But at other times a pretty girl is seen walking along the upper balcony dressed in green. She darts behind one of the support columns, then reappears on the other side. One guide even insists that the "woman in green" pushed him into the pool.

Many staff members believe that this is the spirit of a woman whose Atlantic crossing was never completed — in mortal life at least. Her body was found some forty years ago floating in the pool.

But the "green lady" isn't the only spirit to haunt the pool area. Patsy Laibinis was leading a group of nine tourists when the entire party saw a naval officer in dress whites bedecked with ribbons walk by. Nothing strange about that—except that he was transparent.

The haunted pool.

Los Angeles Area

The *Queen Mary,* located at Pier J at the end of Interstate 710, at Port of Long Beach, is open 365 days a year from 10 a.m. to 6 p. m.. Telephone: (562) 435-3511.

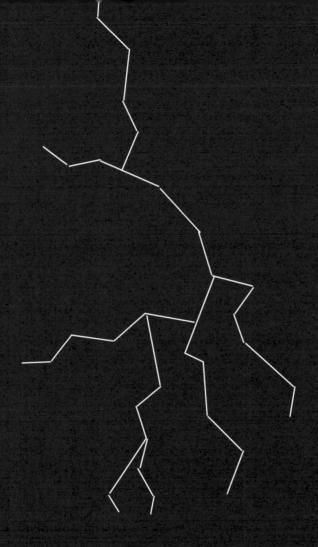

*The ghosts of defunct
bodies fly.*
—Samuel Butler

SAN DIEGO AREA

HOTEL DEL CORONADO

RANCHO JAMUL

HORTON GRAND HOTEL

THOMAS WHALEY HOUSE

CASA DE ESTUDILLO

GRANDE COLONIAL HOTEL

THE FALLBROOK ENTERPRISE

HOTEL DEL CORONADO

THE PRINCE OF WALES, LATER KING OF ENGLAND, FIRST MET his future duchess at a gala hosted in his honor in the grand ballroom of the hotel. The date was April 7, 1920. The former Wallis Simpson, married to a U.S. Naval officer, was a Coronado housewife at the time. The young prince was said to be "nuts" about dancing. It would be more than ten years before the couple really "connected."

In 1920, a movie, *The Flying Fleet*, starring Ramon Navarro and Anita Page, was filmed in the Victorian manorhouse.

In 1958, Billy Wilder chose the hotel as a setting for *Some Like It Hot*, starring Marilyn Monroe, Tony Curtis and Jack Lemmon. Marilyn Monroe, described by the help as a "sweet, quiet lady who ate her one daily meal alone in her room," was merely one superstar in a dazzling chain. Fifty years before, Sarah Bernhardt pronounced the place "Charmante!"

The hotel was also an inspiration for the romantic and highly mystical novel, *Somewhere in Time*—later a movie starring Christopher Reeve.

During the 1890s the hotel management proudly advertised,

> *"There is not any malaria, hay-fever, sleeplessness, loss of appetite, or languor in the air; nor any thunder, lightning, mad dogs, cyclones, heat-terms or cold-snaps—and all these advantages may be enjoyed for $3.00 per day and upward."*

Conspicuously absent was any mention of the hotel's resident ghost.

According to one legend, a young woman guest mysteriously disappeared from Room 502. But another story has the woman — possibly pregnant — committing suicide in that room. In that version, the owner, Elisha Babcock, fearing a scandal, secretly disposed of the corpse, never dreaming that the young lady's spirit would stubbornly refuse to check out.

Year after year her spirit remains, astonishing mortal guests with a variety of poltergeist

Hotel del Coronado. Photograph by C.J. Marrow.

activity. Doors and and windows are said to open and close of their own volition. Footsteps are heard inside the seemingly empty room. Even though Babcock professed not to believe in such "nonsense," he wrote to his son that circumstances had forced him to seal the room.

The ghostly guest has outlasted five successive owners and continues her tenancy to this day. Marcie Buckley, a former employee, reported that other guests have frequently complained of unexpected noises and articles that "move about the room." John Wayne Godown, who works the front desk, tells of some who have demanded to be moved after one night in room 502.

Possibly for this reason, the room is rented only when every other accommodation is filled. Yet security guards roaming the twisting

San Diego Area

fifth floor corridors describe lights that suddenly turn on and off in the unoccupied room.

Besides the ghost, Room 502 boasts one window with a commanding view of the grand hotel's splendid Victorian cupola — except that it's located in the closet. And another strange window — this one facing out into the hall!

To the hotel management this room may be the last resort, but excitement-wise, some guests have rated it quite high.

* * *

Room 502. Note window and closet. Phtograph by C.J. Marrow.

But then along came Alan M. May, a former member of the White House staff *and* a highly successful attorney specializing in murder cases. May was intrigued by the story and determined to find out the truth for himself. First of all, he was certain that room 3502—once 502—was *not* the haunted room.

His reaction was very like my own when he thought the hot, unventilated room with its weird window treatment was more suited to a maid's broom closet than the legendary accommodations assigned "the beautiful stranger" of the legend.

May did some checking and found that the most persistent story involved a woman named either Kate Morgan or Lottie Anderson Bernard. According to the story the woman had arrived at the hotel shortly before Thanksgiving in 1892. Alone and abandoned, She supposedly attempted to abort her unborn child and then shot herself on the ocean veranda of the hotel.

Acting on a hunch the enterprising attorney checked to see if the floor plans had been changed—rooms restructured or renumbered in a major way. Yes, he learned, there had been massive changes at least twice. The search then took him to the Special Collections Division of the Love Library at San Diego State University.

Sure enough, room 3502, thought to have been 502, had really been room 244—a maid's room. The real room 502 is now room 3430. May returned to the hotel and changed rooms, but that night he *still* didn't feel anything.

Certain that he was still in the wrong room, he returned to the library. Turning to the ancient hotel register, he began to thumb through the pages of November 1892 … Thanksgiving …the last Thursday of the month …there on November 24th was a name —Lottie A. Bernard. Checking the room number, he noted that Lottie had been assigned room 302, not 502. Turning to the original floor plans, May found that the room once numbered 302 is now 3312.

On September 2, 1989 the intrepid Alan May checked into room 3312. That night as he lay on the bed in the darkened room looking at the blank screen of the TV set, he became aware of two eyes and a smiling mouth staring at him. May rose, dressed and went out in search of witnesses. He returned with two bellman

San Diego Area

and the elevator operator. They too saw the apparition, the same two eyes; but now the mouth wasn't smiling.

The following day two maintenance engineers came up to check the TV set. The set worked like any other set and there were no eyes, no mouth—smiling or otherwise.   The TV was turned off.

Then, as the two men were leaving the room, the set went back on — of its own accord.

May's next move was a trip to the San Diego Historical Society where he found that the truth was far stranger

Ocean view of Hotel del Coronado. Photo courtesy of hotel.

than the fictionalized legend. A copy of the coroner's inquest held November 30, 1892 revealed that a body had been found on the hotel steps facing the ocean on the previous morning. It was the body of a woman and she had been shot.

A.D. Yomer, the chief clerk, had testified that the dead woman had indeed been a guest and that she'd appeared ill on Thanksgiving day when she checked in—giving her name as Lottie Anderson Bernard. Bernard had asked his advice about her luggage, confiding that her brother, Dr. M. C. Anderson, had been traveling with her but had been called away suddenly leaving her to complete the train trip to San Diego alone. Yomer said that each day until her death, the lady had asked him if her brother had arrived or if a telegram had come from him for her.

The clerk then testified that on the day before she died, he heard from the housekeeper that the lady was ill.   Yomer went to investigate and found her looking very unwell. When he offered to get the house physician, Mrs. Bernard emphatically refused, insisting that her brother would care for her when he arrived.

"I have terminal cancer of the stomach," she confided and then asked him to wire a G. L. Allen of Hamburg, Iowa to okay her draft for more funds.

That night, Yomer said, he sent the wire and the next morning she was found dead. A reply came from Allen saying that her draft for $25 would be honored, but when Yomer wired that Mrs. Bernard had taken her life, there was no response.

Next, the owner of a gunshop testified that a lady dressed in black had come to his gunshop on the afternoon of November 28, 1892 and purchased a gun and cartridges. She was ill and nervous, he said; and, judging from her many anxious questions, appeared to know nothing about guns.

Upon returning to the hotel, May went to the staircase leading to the ocean where the body had

Hotel del Coronado. Photo courtesy of hotel.

been found. The light above the stairs was out. That light was "always" out, a security guard told him. Many electricians had attempted to fix it "but bulbs only last a few nights before they go out."

Continuing his quest at the San Diego Public Library, May found original *San Diego Union* articles regarding the death of the

"Beautiful Stranger," as she was then coming to be known.

> *"Night before last an attractive, prepossessing and highly*
> *educated young woman came down from her room at the*
> *Hotel del Coronado, and between 9 and 10 o'clock*
> *stepped out upon the veranda facing the ocean, which*
> *was lashed into a fury by the tempest that was sweeping*
> *over the whole coast. She was quietly and elegantly*
> *dressed in black, and wore only a shawl over her head.*
> *Nothing more was seen of her until 8:30 yesterday*
> *morning, when the assistant electrician of the hotel,*
> *passing by the end of the western terrace, saw her lying*
> *on the stairs leading to the beach. She was dead............ "*

As the days passed there was much in the press. At first the suicide was attributed to Mrs. Bernard's health, although it developed she described different ailments to the hotel housekeeper, the bellman and the chief clerk. A local physician speculated that her symptoms sounded more like pregnancy than anything else.

Another guest told of having seen Mrs. Bernard on the train that brought her to town. She was traveling with a man and quarreled openly with him, according to the testimony. Though in the end she was heard to say, "I'm sorry, of course you're right," the man left the train in Orange, his manner angry.

Slowly the taut mystery began to unravel. Lottie Bernard was in reality Kate Morgan, the wife of Tom Morgan, a gambler who had changed his name and hers so as not to embarrass his wealthy and socially prominent family.

It's speculated that the "Bernards" worked as a team. Together they rode trains pretending to be a brother and sister. Pretty and young Lottie-Kate attracted suitors. Tom was their entry. To win his favor, they were easily lured into a game of cards. Naturally Tom always won.

Some believe Kate became pregnant and wanted desperately to settle down. While traveling south the couple quarreled. Tom didn't want a child. In the end she relented. She went on to the hotel and there aborted her child for him. Then she waited, lonely and frightened.

It is known that she went to at least one other hotel and inquired if Dr. and Mrs. M. C. Anderson were registered. Then she purchased a gun. The next day she was found dead.

Upon investigation, it was discovered that Kate too came from a wealthy Iowa family. At last a telegram arrived: "Bury her and send me a statement." were the terse instructions. It was sent by Kate's grandfather, J. W. Chandler.

Her husband was never heard from and, two weeks after her death, Kate was buried at Mount Hope Cemetery in San Diego.

But that was not the end of the story. The day after the funeral, the hotel housekeeper, said to be quite distraught about the whole thing, disappeared from *her* room—the old room 502, now known as 3502—the traditionally haunted room.

The stories go on and on. Chris Donovan, the hotel's historian tries to sort them out. "I feel a responsibility to record the sighting correctly—in a manner that's not complicated by personal experience. Though I embrace the concept of spirits, I've never seen Kate or any ghostly manifestation. Perhaps that makes it easier to investigate her sightings."

Donovan's found that those who report seeing ghosts fall into two categories. "Some are afraid of sounding strange. They'll ask a random question of an employee— something very discrete. I'll sense they've seen something and start asking questions. Sometimes I have to drag the story out of them. Others are in your face about it. They just have to share. 'I saw a girl on my way to the tour bus. She disappeared before my eyes.' Or 'Something moved my shoes around.' Now, I ask you, who would make up stories like that?"

It's been well over a hundred years since Kate's death. Many wonder what keeps her at the Hotel Del, but not Donovan. "There are surely worse places to spend eternity," she points out.

Veranda of Hotel del Coronado at the time of Kate Morgan's disappearance.

"Kate was estranged from her family. Perhaps she had no where to go. Besides, hotels are special. Unlike a warehouse or theater, a hotel is a home away from home."

Whatever the case, it appears that Kate feels proprietary about the hotel. Mary Lundeen, who manages the gift shop, is certain that Kate is jealous of Marilyn Monroe.

Lundeen's shop is filled with Monroe paraphernalia commemorating the Some Like It Hot association. On four different occasions

Marilyn Monroe coffee mugs have flown off the shelf in full view of customers and landed right side up on the counter. "I don't think Kate likes Marilyn getting all that attention," Lundeen speculates.

Once night the manager saw a woman strolling the shop arcade in old fashioned clothing. On other occasions she's come in and found merchandise askew when she'd left it in perfect order the previous day.

Mary Lundeen's Marilyn Monroe mugs seem to annoy Kate.

"Kate's a little mischievous—putting my dictionaries and thesauruses in backwards or upside down," Lundeen says. "I'm sure that's her way of saying 'I'm still here, I'm still here.'"

Karin Lekas of Irvine, CA was part of a four-couple group celebrating a birthday at the Hotel Del. When Lekas returned to her room after dinner, she glanced at a the door next to hers and saw a beautiful woman standing in the doorway. "She looked. I looked. She smiled. I smiled. She went into her room. I went into my room."

Realizing suddenly what she'd seen, Lekas whirled around. The vision had vanished. "People think of ghosts as sad or scary but the 'Kate' I saw was happy and beautiful," Lekas explains. "She had long dark hair pulled up and was wearing a lovely dress with a fitted waist, high collar with tucks down the front and sheer sleeves in a voile-like fabric. But there was no color to her or her clothes—as if there was no life."

The experience was so real to Lekas that she immediately sat down and sketched the ghost that she had seen.

CCM, an anesthetist vacationing from Mooresville, North Carolina, was admiring the sea view from her window when she was surprised to see a woman wearing Victorian.

San Diego Area

clothing strolling the beach. As she watched, the woman turned and looked directly at her. The next day CCM purchased a book about the hotel's history which gave the specific location where Kate's body had been found. The strange woman had been walking in Kate's exact footsteps.

Richard Rodriguez thought his wife, Jennifer, a history teacher, would be delighted with a Valentine's Day stay at the Hotel del. He specifically asked for a room in the Victorian Tower. That evening as Jennifer was taking a shower, the bathroom light began to flicker on and off. Later as she lay on the bed waiting for her husband to finish his shower, she saw the tassel on the room's ceiling fan begin to move as though someone had walked by and brushed it.

"I didn't tell Richard," she recalls. "He was so cynical in those days. He didn't even believe in God. I was sure he'd laugh at me for imagining anything weird going on."

Later, as the couple slept, their bedcovers were jerked off the bed. Jennifer thought her husband was hogging the blankets and went back to sleep. In the morning he startled her by asking, "Did you see what happened last night?" She had no idea what he was talking about.

Richard told Jennifer that their covers had been pulled off by a woman standing at the foot of the bed. As though that weren't enough, the doorknob began to rattle at the same time. Though drawn to find out what was causing the noise, Rodriguez was too frightened to get out of bed.

Only then did Jennifer tell him about seeing the swaying tassel. To her surprise, Richard told her that he'd seen the same thing as he lay sleepless throughout the long night.

Jennifer said a prayer for what she imagined to be the room's troubled spirit. Richard called the desk and asked for a bellman to

Turret view of Hotel del Coronado. Photo courtesy of hotel.

help them move to another room. "How did it feel to sleep in the haunted room?" the bellman asked on arrival. It was the first time the couple had any idea that the room was considered haunted.

Three weeks later the Rodriguez's were discussing their experiences at the Del, when the phone rang. A representative of San Diego's Old Globe Theatre was calling to inform them that they'd won the grand prize in a contest: a weekend at the Hotel del Coronado.

The couple was delighted but made it clear: any room but 3327

Still, Jennifer wouldn't have traded the original experience. "I take my hat off to Kate Morgan. She did something that I couldn't do—Kate got my husband going to church."

The Hotel del Coronado is located 1500 Orange Dr. Coronado 92118. Tel: 619 435-2181 Fax 522 8491 www.hoteldel.com

San Diego Area

RANCHO JAMUL

SOME HISTORIANS BELIEVE THE NAME "JAMUL" MEANT WATER of the antelope. Some say it meant good water, while others insist that it's just the ancient Indian word for slimy water.

But no matter what kind of water it was, there was plenty of it there in 1829 when Pio Pico received his 8,926 acre grant from the governor of California. It was a splendid windfall even for those open-handed times.

Rancho Jamul in the mid-15th century.
Photograph courtesy of the Historical Collection of the Title Insurance and Trust.

An imposing hacienda was built, cattle stocked, and before long the rancho was a showplace. Then, in 1837, while Pico was away and his mother and three unmarried sisters were staying at the rancho, an Indian servant warned the family that neighboring Indians were massing for an attack. The Pico family fled; but their majordomo, Juan Leiva, remained with his family.

It was a tragic mistake. Leiva's son, Jose, was killed almost immediately by Indians as were the other *vaqueros*. Juan Leiva, though wounded, was able to stagger to the gun room just in time to see an Indian servant lock the door and run away. He was finally reduced to defending his family by flinging coals from the fireplace at the advancing Indians.

Approach to Rancho Jamul.
Photograph by C.J. Marrow.

His courageous stand was useless. Leiva was slaughtered; his wife, Doña Maria, and their young son were stripped and then abandoned in the wilderness. The proud Pico estate was set afire, the house totally destroyed. Doña Maria had watched helplessly as her two teenage daughters were carried away by the Indians. She and her small son then walked the twenty-one miles to San Diego barefoot and naked.

An expedition was sent to rescue the girls. The small but determined force searched for three months. Once, the Indians were overtaken. The girls could be seen in the distance, their bodies smeared with white paint, their hair cut Indian fashion. Many were killed in the battle that followed but the surviving Indians dragged the screaming girls back into the hills.

When the contingent returned to San Diego, Doña Maria was dead. The violent tragedy had simply proved too much for her. Though a large reward was offered for the recovery of the Leiva girls, they were never seen again.

And that's only one story connected with Rancho Jamul—now one of the largest cattle ranches in the state. During the 1870's tragedy again erupted. California was part of the United States now

San Diego Area

Rancho Jamul as it is today. Photograph by C.J. Marrow.

and many of the greedy newcomers felt that fact gave them precedence over the Spanish-speaking natives. Hoards of squatters descended upon the place.

The Mexican-American owners of Rancho Jamul took their claim to the Supreme Court and won, but that was not the end of their problems by any means. The squatters simply refused to budge.

Over the years the rancho was the scene of blood feuds and a series of grisly unresolved murders —squatters found with their heads bashed in. According to one legend the murderer was discovered and immediately lynched by an angry mob. When the authorities arrived, the body had disappeared. It was never found.

Generations of ranch hands at Jamul have told of apparitions, lights, cold spots, the cries of Indians and the screams of women. Some refuse to venture into certain areas of the sprawling ranch.

The second Pico home, built in 1852 and elegantly modernized in recent years, is owned today by Lawrence and Bertha Daley.

"People are always seeing things, hearing things," Bertha Daley says. "I often stay here alone but never *feel* alone. Whatever's here must like me and I certainly like it — or them. We have an understanding, I think — a mutual respect. The vicious tragedies of the past have left their imprint. One feels it, of course, but history is a continuing thing that unfolds from day to day. I feel the past. I'm aware of it every day, but I still live very much in the now."

Rancho Jamul is located at 14726 Campo Road, Jamul.

THE HORTON GRAND HOTEL

VERN APPLEBY WAS ONE OF THOSE NO NONSENSE TYPES. Hardly the sort to believe in ghosts, but that was before he spent a night at San Diego's historic Horton Grand.

He thought nothing of sleeping in 309 — the notorious haunted room — nothing until he was awakened at midnight by someone, some*thing* tugging at the mattress seemingly intent on literally pulling the bed out from under him.

Members of the Horton staff are used to hearing such stories. " It's just Roger doing his number again," they said.

Roger, it seems, was a gambler shot by his fiance's father while hiding in an armoire. Of course the tragedy didn't occur at the Horton Grand. It didn't even happen in the handsome antique armoire that graces room 309. But that shouldn't seem strange, nothing about the showplace hotel is quite what it seems.

The Horton Grand is really two hotels with two very different histories. From the street, the left wing is a confection of gingerbread and icing, while the right, though of the same vintage, has square, spare, lines Connecting the two is a glass atrium. Inside, a restaurant, its   ambience dark, velvety, romantic, is named Ida Bailey's after the city's most fashionable madam whose plush bordello once stood on the very spot.

Even without its resident ghost, the Horton Grand is certainly one of the most unusual hotels in the county. The eccentric charmer is actually two hostelries in one, comprised of the two oldest in San Diego moved to their present location.

San Diego Area

The Horton Grand Hotel. Photograph courtesy of the hotel.

During the late 1970s, construction of the Horton Plaza shopping extravaganza which now anchors the newly renovated downtown area, threatened the old Horton Grand. Developer Dan Pearson was appalled. This had once been the fanciest hotel in town. So what if it had degenerated into a flophouse. So what if the City Council had voted to demolish it. Something had to be done.

The something turned out to be moving the building brick by brick. Pearson bought the doomed inn for $1, found a prime location (the site of the famed bordello) only two blocks from Horton Plaza and bought it. Five months later the old hotel lay in 10,000 numbered pieces in a warehouse.

There they languished until 1982 when Pearson learned that the Salvation Army, which owned the Kahle Saddlery Hotel,was going to tear it down.

The Saddlery, a *"Cowboy Victorian,"* had once been the home of Wyatt Earp. Could Pearson allow so much history to go the way of a parking lot? Of course not.

The Saddlery, with its old west persona, was moved, and the Horton Grand reconstructed by its side. And there they are today, at once swaggering and perfumed, reminiscent of both clanking spurs and lilting laughter. Dan Pearson has taken the ghosts of Wyatt and Ida and pronounced them man and mistress.

Ida Bailey's in the Horton Grand Hotel. Photograph courtesy of the hotel.

That's just the beginning. The $12 million reconstruction project was completed in 1986, the hundredth anniversary of both progenitors. And then strange things began to happen.

The hotel had scarcely been open ten days before Martha Mayes, one of the maids, appeared in Pearson's office complaining that something was going on in room 309. As time passed it got to the point where employees would insist on going in only in twos or threes. No one wanted to be there alone. How can you concentrate on cleaning when lights go on and off by themselves or objects move—seemingly of their own volition?

Mayes, now a bookkeeper at the hotel, says, "It went on for about a year before anyone would take us seriously. The beds would

San Diego Area

Haunted room in the Horton Grand Hotel.
Photograph courtesy of the hotel.

shake, closet doors would fly open. Once a guest stopped a man in the hall to inquire where the ice machine was and he faded away right before her eyes."

In November 1987 Shelly Deegan, a San Diego psychic, was called in. Deegan believes the whole hotel is haunted, but says the most active spirit is that of Roger Whittaker, the gambler who ended his life in an armoire similar to the one in Room 309. "Nothing in the hotel has any connection with his life," she says, "he just likes the ambience. Who wouldn't enjoy hanging out at the Horton Grand?"

A month later Chris McGuire, Kiwanis Club president and an administrative assistant at a rival hotel, asked if she might celebrate her birthday, December 14, 1987, in the haunted room. It was arranged.

"There were six of us," McGuire says. "We checked out the room for awhile, then decided to go out for dinner. When we tried to leave, the door stuck at the top. It had opened normally when we arrived, but when we wanted to leave, we had to pull very hard to get out.

"Returning later, we found that things had been moved around. Well, of course someone might have been playing a trick—but what happened afterwards, how could that be a trick?" Sleeping alone in the room, McGuire was awakened twice by someone touching her upper arm. "The third time I opened my eyes to see a kind of mist beside me. I felt that something was trying to pull me toward it. At the same time the bed seemed to be vibrating. As I screamed it all just faded away."

But that certainly wasn't the end of Roger. On October 31, 1991 a local radio station decided to do a Halloween special at the hotel. When a coffin was brought in as a promotion, the desk clerk jokingly apologized: "Sorry, Roger, don't be upset. It's just for the night, the coffin won't be staying."

Suddenly, in full view of four people, a legal sized clipboard that had been wedged behind the credit

Atrium connecting the Horton Grand Hotel and the Saddlery. Photograph courtesy of the hotel.

card machine flew straight up in the air and sailed four feet across the room before crashing to the ground beside the coffin.

It appears obvious Roger was making a statement. Coffins are not to his taste. Here's a ghost who likes to be where the action is. For whatever reason, Roger's checked himself into the Horton Grand and has no intention of leaving feet first.

The Horton Grand Hotel is located at 311 Island Avenue, San Diego 92101. Telephone: (619) 544-1886.

San Diego Area

THOMAS WHALEY HOUSE

FUNERAL HUMOR OCCUPIES A VERY SPECIAL PLACE WITHIN the human consciousness. No matter how sophisticated the culture or the individual, the need remains to render death less fearful with a little tentative ridicule. Perhaps laughter is itself an affirmation of life. Macabre jokes are always in vogue.

The Thomas Whaley House. Photograp by A. May.

A perennial favorite is the one about the boy who disrupts mourners at a burial service by rushing about crying, "Programs! Programs! Get your programs! You can't tell the dead ones from the lives ones without a program!"

For the late June Reading, director of the historic Whaley House in San Diego, the problem of determining the lives ones is no joke. After more than thirty years in a haunted house, she takes the apparitions that inhabit the showplace in her stride—though, admittedly, it's confusing to see someone wandering about and not know whether she or he is a living ticket holder or a spectre from the original cast.

Current fashions only add to the confusion. That exotic dark-haired woman standing before the bench in a flamboyant outfit could be the spirit of a fandango girl hauled into court—when the Whaley House doubled as a courthouse—for hustling too aggressively. Those two young girls fluttering about the upstairs bedroom in their gingham granny gowns might be the Whaley daughters who once caused the house to echo with th sound of their treadle sewing machine. And the tall, mustachioed man in a dark coat and vest standing at the top of the stairs, couldn't that be Thomas Whaley himself?

Thomas Whaley

The late June Reading has sometimes thought so.

* * *

The Whaley House, built in 1857, was once the grand mansion of a frontier town. The very walls seem charged with passion, violence, fear and anger, rendered even more impressive by the knowledge that the house was built on a site used for public executions. How much unfinished business still remains can only be judged by the number of restless spirits seen by visitors and caretakers and by the frequency of their appearances.

The story of Thomas Whaley, the man who built the house, is—in part—the saga of San Diego itself. As the son of an early American pioneer family grown to prosperity, a life of conventional ease at the helm of the family business in New York seemed to stretch before him like a plush Victorian carpet. Then a stray headline caught his eye. It was the year 1848. A tea caddy

San Diego Area

of nuggets had been presented to President Polk, glittering evidence of gold in California.

At twenty-five, young Whaley was ripe for adventure, eager to make his own way in an exciting new world. He was among the first wave of adventurers to reach California, focusing on commerce rather than mining.

During the extremely hazardous 204-day voyage around Cape Horn, the young man's thoughts were of the sweetheart he'd left behind. Writing home to his mother, he suggested, "You might call on Mrs. De Lannay; you will find her a very pleasant lady. I may as well inform you that I have a particular regard for her youngest daughter, Miss Anna; indeed I love her and intend marrying her if I ever return from California a rich man."

Growing impatient, he added, "I may send for her. She is a pleasant and amiable young lady of very affectionate disposition and gentle and innocent as a lamb. She is only sixteen years of age. You would no doubt love her as a daughter-in-law..."

To Anna, he glowingly described a thriving village and nightly fandango dances but discreetly omitted the fact that San Diego was under marshal law as a result of frequent Indian attacks. Between battles, Thomas wrote, "Not a night passes, Anna, but that I look at your daguerreotype ... sleep with it under my pillow. . .It gives me great pleasure to gaze upon it... You may have grown tall, and adopted the 'Bloomer Costume'... If that were the case I should not know you... I am ready to take you for better or worse, so it makes no difference in what shape you appear so long as you come."

The courtship—conducted entirely by mail—lasted five years. Thomas returned to New York, married Anna and brought her back with him to San Diego. Soon he began construction of what would one day be known as the Whaley House. It was, he wrote home to mother, "the nicest place in San Diego." As the years

passed many dig-
nitaries enjoyed
the hospitality of
the Whaley
home, including
Presidents Grant
and Harrison.

Later the county
leased a portion
of the home to
be used as a
courthouse for

Courtroon, Whaley House. Photograph by C.J. Marrow.

$65 a month. One large room was set aside for the courtroom and
three upstairs rooms for storage of county records. Frontier justice
was dispensed there for several years.

Then, as new settlers began to pour into the area, the population
of San Diego shifted from Old Town—where the Whaley House
was located. New Towners became increasingly demanding,
insisting that county offices and records be moved to a more
central location. Whaley and other Old Town dignitaries
stubbornly refused to yield. Finally an order was obtained to seize
the records and county furniture.

Incensed, the people of Old Town announced that any effort to
remove the records would be met with rifle fire. Once again
marshal law was declared in Old Town. The Whaley House was
sandbagged for protection and militant residents carried six-guns.
"Old Town has seceded!" the San Diego Union announced in
bold headlines following the placement of a cannon before the
Whaley House.

Tensions lessened as no immediate effort was made to enforce the
order. Whaley decided that it was safe to make a quick business
trip to San Francisco. At midnight, following his departure, the
opposing forces greased their rented Wells Fargo wagons, muffled

their horses' hoofs with gunny sacks and headed for the Whaley House. There the armed party forced its way insjde and stopped Anna at gunpoint on the ninth step of the stairway leading to the record storage room.

Hearing the sound of footsteps, six-year-old Lillian Whaley jumped out of bed believing that her father had returned unexpectedly. Running to greet him, she was confronted by the sight of her tiny 4' 11" mother surrounded by armed men. Though Lillian lived to be a very old woman, she never forgot the incident.

And neither would Whaley who was greeted by the accomplished fact upon his return a few days later. Learning that his beloved wife had been threatened, his castle invaded, and a goodly source of revenue removed, Whaley was furious. Indignantly, he penned numerous letters to the board demanding rent and repairs on the building which had been damaged by the break-in. The fact that the lease had not expired, leaving the county clearly liable, was blatantly ignored by everyone but Whaley. His requests that the action be reviewed were denied. Again and again his angry letters were "tabled for future consideration."

Though the glory years were over, the lusty pioneer had no intention of admitting defeat. He continued litigation until his death nineteen years later. The affair was never settled. Anna Whaley died in 1913; but Lillian, who had witnessed the dramatic scene as a small child, lived on in the family home until her own death in 1953—just nine days short of her ninetieth birthday.

In 1956, the Board of Supervisors of the County of San Diego vindicated itself to some degree by purchasing the then dilapidated dwelling which was slated for destruction. The house was restored and refurnished and is now maintained by the Historical Shrine Foundation.

But that's only the beginning of the story.

* * *

Almost immediately the late June Reading, who was active in directing the renovation of the home, was aware of some mysterious, unexplain- ed presence. It began with footsteps. She recalls a morning when she arrived at the house early intending to furnish the upstairs rooms. "Two men were with me," she explains. "They were county workmen who were painting some shelving in the hall. Suddenly we heard the distinct sound of someone walking in the bedroom above us. I assumed that it

June Reading at the Thomas Whaley House with the mysterious rocking chair. Photograph by C.J. Marrow.

must be another workman who'd arrived ahead of us, but when I went up to investigate there was no one there. One of the men joked about spirits coming in to look things over and promptly forgot the matter. That was such a busy time—the house was to be opened to the public in just one week.

"However, the sound of walking continued. And for the next six months I found myself going upstairs again and again to see if someone was actually there. This would happen during the day, sometimes when

visitors were in other parts of *Ghostly silhouette in center and right hand corner.* the house, or at other times when I was busy at my desk trying to catch up on correspondence or bookwork. At times it would sound as if someone was descending the stairs, but the steps would fade away before reaching the first floor.

"The next thing we knew the windows in the upper part of the house began to assert themselves, opening seemingly of their own volition. We installed horizontal bolts on three windows in the front bedroom, thinking that would end the matter. It didn't. The really annoying part of it all came when the opening of the windows set off our burglar alarm in the middle of the night. Frequently we were called by the police and the San Diego Burglar Alarm Company to come and see if the house had been broken into. Only once did we find any evidence of human disturbance."

Then, while giving a talk to twenty-five school children, Reading again heard the sound of someone walking. The footsteps seemed to come from the roof. After one of the children interrupted to ask what the noise was, she went outside to see if a county repairman might be working on the roof. There was no one in sight.

It soon came to light that residents of Old Town were familiar with this sound. It had been a neighborhood phenomenon for many years. Lillian Whaley had often complained of it during her long lifetime in the house. Neighbors also told of how a large, heavy china closet had tipped over seemingly of its own volition in 1912, one year before the death of Anna Whaley.

Before long a colorful parade of apparitions began to appear. Grace Boruquin, a volunteer guide at the house, looked up one afternoon and saw the figure of a man on the staircase, clad in a frock coat and pantaloons.

A Mrs. Kirby, wife of the Director of the Medical Association of New Westminster, B.C., who was visiting the house, saw an apparition of a woman in the courtroom. She described the woman as small and dark skinned, wearing a calico dress with a long full skirt reaching to the floor and gold hoops in her pieced ears. The spirit's eyes and hair were dark. "I got the impression that she lives here and we are sort of invading her privacy," the astonished tourist confided.

Next Suzanne Pere of El Cajon, California reported seeing a kind of spectral town meeting. "There was a group of men in the study dressed in frock coats," she said. "One had a thick gold watch chain across his vest. It seemed to be a very lively discussion; all the figures were animated, some pacing the floor, others conversing; all serious and agitated, oblivious to everything else. One figure in the group seemed to be an official and stood off by himself. This person was of medium stocky build, had light brown hair, and a mustache which was quite full and long. He had very piercing light blue eyes and a penetrating gaze. He seemed about to speak."

Many who have visited the house have reported hearing deep, baritone laughter, smelling cologne and/or cigar smoke, and feeling pressure upon themselves while climbing the stairs as though something were trying to prevent their progress. One woman felt herself literally forced out of an upstairs bedroom by unseen hands.

Then the famous English medium Sybil Leek was invited to visit the Whaley House in the hope that she might be able to make contact with its discarnate inhabitants. TV personality Regis Philbin and a camera crew were on hand to record the event. Disavowing any knowledge of the past history of the house—the trials of Thomas Whaley or the recent psychic disturbances—the medium, who had just flown in for the occasion, proceeded to communicate with a troubled male spirit who muttered resentfully of people in the house. Speaking through Sybil's lips, the entity told of an injustice perpetrated upon him and demanded redress.

The words coincided exactly with letters written ninety years before by Thomas Whaley which had never been placed on public display. When the spirit's angry harangue was played back via tape recorder, the forceful intonations of the voice exactly matched the imprint of a quill pen at various heated passages in the correspondence. Splashes of ink testified to the indignant

San Diego Area

emphasis of the writer coinciding exactly with the forceful exclamations of the speaker.

The spirit then told of opening the windows and triggering the alarm bell, thereby causing the police to come. This was a means of calling attention to himself, he explained, of showing the world that he was still master of the house. Sybil had not been given any of this background information, nor could she possibly have known the maiden name of Anna Whaley which was imparted to her by the spirit. "Anna Lannay plays the organ," she understood him to say.

Contact was also made with another spirit, one who complained of a bad fever, talked of "confusion" around him and begged for a drink of water. This manifestation was later related to a tragic occurrence which had taken place in 1852 when the land which would later accommodate the Whaley House was used as a place of execution. It involved a man by the name of Yankee Jim Robinson who had jumped ship and stolen a boat. The runaway sailor was merely rowing about the bay sightseeing when apprehended. In attempting to escape, Robinson was wounded in a sabre duel. The injury didn't heal; and, while languishing in jail, he became seriously ill. The unfortunate man was dragged into court while suffering a raging fever and remained unconscious throughout much of the trial.

When the drunken judge pronounced sentence — death by hanging — Jim thought it was merely a bad joke intended to teach him a lesson. Dazed by his illness, he continued in his wishful thinking until the execution wagon was pulled out from under him and he dangled from a rope. To add to the agony of the moment, the scaffold was too short for Yankee Jim's long legs. Instead of his neck being broken instantly, he was allowed to slowly strangle to death. The cruel death took forty-five minutes and was never forgotten by the witnesses who told of his anguished curses.

The scaffold had stood in the place where an arch now divides the music room of the Whaley House from the front parlor. Many consider this a cold, fearsome spot without knowing its gruesome history. In 1935, Lillian Whaley told a reporter from the *San Diego Union* that her father had once rented the house temporarily to tenants who were so frightened by the presence of Yankee Jim that they had the house exorcised.

One who claims to have seen Yankee Jim in recent times is Kay Sterner, a retired school teacher with psychic ability, who visited the house at the request of the late June Reading. Sterner, who is the founder of the California Parapsychology Foundation, knew nothing of the Whaley House or its previous occupants.

While approaching the house the gifted medium was suddenly aware of a primitive scaffold with a man hanging from it. A team of mules had just pulled a wagon from beneath the struggling body. The scene appeared to be superimposed on the house itself and Sterner was able to point out that the spectral scaffold was erected on the site of the arch between the music room and the living room, a fact verified by county records.

Clairvoyantly, Kay Sterner was able to "see" an old coach house — long since gone — and a wagon with two horses standing in the backyard. The description was later confirmed. In the courtroom inside the Whaley House, she saw a rowdy group of sailors, prostitutes and apparent bandits taking their turns before the bench. The atmosphere seemed charged with tension as they continued to replay some dramatic episode of more than one hundred years ago.

One of the most evidential of the sightings was that of a stocky man wearing boots and carrying a log hook. He appeared to be disturbed and Sterner picked up the fact that he was upset about a case that he had adjudicated. He was a highly scrupulous man, she said, and seemed to suffer from a leg injury.

The late June Reading later informed her that this description matched that of Squire A.R. Ensworth, who had been Whaley's lawyer and business manager, and also a magistrate. Reading showed the medium letters indicating great concern on Ensworth's part as to whether he had made the right decision in a specific case involving Whaley. She also revealed that the lawyer had fallen into a hole on the property and broken his leg. It had never been properly set.

Possible ectoplasm in upper left hand corner.

Even more dramatic was the reenactment before the medium's very eyes of a brutal murder. The phenomenon began with loud, agonizing screams. Then she saw a Mexican woman with long flowing dark hair, a bright blouse and long ruffled skirt run shrieking down the hall. She was pursued by a man of dark complexion who accused her of being unfaithful. There was a violent quarrel and Sterner watched in helpless terror as the man drew a knife and slashed his errant love to death. Later she learned from Reading that a heated quarrel between a Mexican couple had ended with the wife's stabbing. The tragedy had occurred in the upstairs bedroom as the medium had seen it.

Another sad event witnessed by Sterner and then verified by the historian was the death of a small child. The medium "saw" this taking place in the room where the Whaley son had died at seventeen months.

The final apparition revealed clairvoyantly was that of a woman wearing a nightgown and cap making the rounds of the house, checking to see if the children were asleep, the windows fastened and the doors bolted. One might assume that Mrs. Whaley — like her husband — still holds a proprietary claim upon an earthly status symbol.

So much verifiable information coming from psychic sources does seem to corroborate the legends of the house as well as the current manifestations that seem all in a day's work to the late June Reading and her assistants. The years pass and the stories persist. The smell of Thomas Whaley's favorite cigar floats down the corridors, a ghostly gavel echoes, a rocker unaccountably begins to rock.

The haunted arch at the Whaley House. Photograph by C.J. Marrow.

Many decades have passed since the museum's opening in 1960. Gary Beck, who was first drawn to the house's haunted history as a boy, has become its new director. Beck has his own tales to tell. He's heard the old family music box—a hand cranked instrument—suddenly begin to play of its own accord. He's seen a meat cleaver begin to swing—in mid air. On many occasions he's heard footsteps over head when no one—at least no alive—was upstairs. In fact, Beck believes he can tell the difference between Thomas Whaley's footsteps and Yankee Jim's. Yankee Jim's are much heavier. Dean Glass, who also works at the museum, opened the door one winter morning in 2005 and was startled by a figure at the top of the stairwell. "He was looking straight at me," Glass says, "and then he just slowly disappeared." Later Glass came upon an old photograph of Thomas Whaley as a twenty-year-old. "I knew instantly that was the man I'd seen." And so it seems that fresh history mingles with old. New wonder tales are collected as visitors suddenly catch glimpses of spirits who apparently find life in the Whaley House just too exciting to leave behind.

The Whaley House, recognized by the State of California as an "Official Haunted House," is open every day but Wednesday. It is located at 2482 San Diego Ave., San Diego 92110 Telephone: (619) 297-9327.

San Diego Area

CASA DE ESTUDILLO

CASA DE ESTUDILLO, THE GRAND DAME OF SAN DIEGO'S Old Town has gone through many vicissitudes.   Built in 1829 by the dashing 26 year old José Antonio Estudillo, the house— which would be used as a fort during the Mexican-American War— was designed as a show place for his wife, Maria Victoria.

Casa de Estudillo today. Photograph by A. May.

As was the custom with grand mansions, the four foot adobe walls were coated with whitewash and the tile roof layered over with mud, matted seaweed and reeds supported by rough rafters bound together by leather thongs. The twelve spacious rooms opening directly onto the central courtyard included a chapel and a grand sala where balls were held.

The son of the former commander of the San Diego presidio and one of the wealthiest landowners in the region, Estudillo served in the military and later as the town's revenue collector and treasurer. When the American government was established, he was appointed county treasurer and assessor. In addition to Old Town property—a prime piece of real estate in the center of town—he held title land grants in Temecula, San Jacinto, San Juan Capistrano and the Otay Rancho.

For years the house was a social mecca, accommodating not only the Estudillos' eleven children, but frequent guests from all over the state. Widowed in 1852, Maria Estudillo not only kept the family together but added to it by adopting nine orphaned relatives and several Indian children whose parents had died.

After the matriarch's death the Estudillo clan resided in the house until 1887 when the last family member moved out. That might have been the end of the story—but wasn't.

* * *

In 1882 Helen Hunt Jackson, an immensely successful novelist and frustrated crusader, had come to San Diego to seek information regarding the mistreatment of the Mission Indians. She found a kindred spirit in Father Anthony Ubach, a cigar-smoking militant with an outspoken tongue and a strong taste for Spanish wine, who lived in the Estudillo home and maintained a community chapel there.

The soldier-style priest who angrily protested the treatment of the Indians whose responsibility he'd shouldered was delighted to find a potential ally in the equally outspoken Eastern writer. Ubach regaled Jackson with stories of San Diego and its colorful past. One that left a lasting impression was about a young couple who had appeared at his door late one night. The woman was the daughter of a prominent California family, the man an Indian sheepherder. They begged him to marry them immediately, which he did. Soon after, the couple was apprehended by the bride's angry family. The union was annulled, the woman subsequently forced into marriage with another, and the Indian beaten nearly to death. It was tragic, romantic, a tale a writer would not forget ...

* * *

Casa de Esttudillo.

Helen Hunt Jackson's *Ramona* was acclaimed the great American novel; and, as a result, a far reaching mystique was born—much of it commercial. Published in 1884, the book has been reprinted more than 300 times, been translated widely, made into four movies, countless plays and pageants; and lent its name to cities, streets, songs and products. Thirty-two years later it was deemed a conservative estimate that *Ramona* had been worth $50,000,000 in tourist revenue to Southern California.

Never out of print, *Ramona* continues to sell briskly, influencing thousands to visit the sites described. Because the story is essentially a romantic one, the scene of the protagonist's wedding was of immediate fascination. It did no good for the publisher to protest that the plot was a fabrication. Readers simply wouldn't believe that Ramona wasn't real. The idea of her elopement with the handsome Indian, Alessandro, simply had to be true. Surely the chapel where they exchanged vows must exist somewhere in San Diego.

Speculation quickly centered around the Estudillo home. Avid researchers decided that since no Catholic Church existed in San Diego's Old Town at the time of the Ramona episode, any marriage would have to have been performed in the chapel of the abandoned Estudillo home where community masses were celebrated and Father Ubach had actually lived. Soon the caretaker was doing a brisk business selling bits of wood and tile ripped from the walls to tourists who believed that Ramona had really been married there.

A promise that the property would always be known as Casa de Estudillo and $500 bought the crumbling adobe in 1906. Within a year the place had changed hands again, this time for only $10. John Spreckels, the new owner, who also owned the Hotel del Coronado and the San Diego Electric Railway Line, had a grand design. His hotel guests needed something more than the beach and he needed a terminus for his railroad. The Ramona legend solved both problems.

Hazel Waterman, San Diego's first woman architect, was hired to restore the building to its former glory. The result was an exquisitely restored mansion, but what Spreckels wanted was a tourist mecca. He decorated the chapel with Indian style trinkets and brought in a minister to marry couples in the same spot that Ramona and Alessandro supposedly had stood. Souvenirs were sold in an adjoining shop and outside in the courtyard hopefuls tossed pennies into a wishing well. The enterprise was a dazzling success from the very beginning. Four movies and a steady stream of tourists continued to swell attendance.

Then in 1968, Legler Benbough, a civic leader, purchased the property and deeded it to the State of California. The San Diego chapter of the Colonial Dames of America took on the task of refurnishing the historic adobe with early California antiques.

After much controversy, the name, "Ramona's Marriage Place," was finally dropped from the museum show place. It took more than sixty years, but a promise was finally honored. The place is once again known as Casa de Estudillo.

* * *

But that's not the end of the story either. Members of the museum staff have reported a series of strange experiences. Faces suddenly appear in mirrors—faces that are not reflections. The lid on a music box in the Blue Room once rose of its own accord and music began to play. Shadowy figures appear to glide across the floor.

San Diego Area

In an effort to record this mystifying phenomena, Sandy Pavicic, a reporter from the *Riverside Press Enterprise*, Brian Black and Don Walther undertook an investigation of the museum on a sunny day in April 1988. Brian Black, who had turned on his tape recorder, was leading the way as they entered the second room, a study. As he stepped inside, he felt as though he'd walked into someone or something.

Suddenly Black felt himself "racked from head to toe with a cold and tingly sensation." He turned quickly and exited, but Pavicic and Walther continued into the room only to encounter the same chilly resistance. It was then that Sandy Pavicic saw flashes of red light in the adjacent master bedroom. None of them could find a reflection or other light source to cause such an occurrence.

Walther was carrying Pavicic's camera case under his right arm. It contained a variety of filters and telephoto lenses. With dramatic suddenness, the party was startled by a loud crash. Somehow Pavicic's most expensive telephoto lens had gotten out of the camera case without its lens cap and hit the concrete floor hard enough to shear off part of the interface between camera and lens.

Black had been watching at the time and was certain that Walther had not tipped the case. Upon investigation, it was noted that the storage compartment for the lens was located deep inside the case and held the lens snugly. When they experimented by holding the case upside down and shaking it, they found that the lens wouldn't come loose.

Adding to the mystery was a missing lens cap that was neither on the floor or inside the case. Though Pavicic had checked her equipment carefully that morning and was certain that everything was in place, the cap was nowhere to be found.

But an even stranger discovery awaited them when Black played his tape. Just seconds before the lens hit the floor, the sound of plastic twisting against metal can be heard distinctly. After experimenting, they were able to determine that this was the same sound as that made by the removal of a lens cap from a telephoto lens.

Even more dramatic was a gruff male voice picked up by the recorder shortly after the lens hit the floor. *"Get out! "* it demands.

It would appear that the trio had trespassed on some entity's psychic space. Perhaps the light flashes, the broken lens and the missing cap were all a means of displaying proprietary anger.

And just who does the mysterious spirit voice belong to? Could it perhaps be Father Ubach? Or possibly the original patriarch José Antonio Estudillo? Perhaps *you'll* be the one to discover the truth.

Casa Estudillo is located in the Old Town State Park at 4002 Wallis. Phone: (619) 220-5426.

GRANDE COLONIAL HOTEL

LA JOLLA'S GRANDE COLONIAL HOTEL HAS BEEN WHERE THE action is for a very long time. The seaside town's oldest hotel, the Grande Colonial opened in 1913 and has been full of spirited activity ever since.

Grande Colonial Hotel 1928. Courtesy of the Grande Colonial La Jolla.

The hotel is grand—small wonder spirits don't want to leave. At least that's what Lisa Riley, formerly the hotel's executive administrative assistant, thinks. Riley used to come in at five every morning because she liked quiet time alone to get things done. The trouble is, the hotel isn't always so quiet. She heard voices when there was no one there, heard footsteps where was no one's walking—no one that she could see anyway.

One morning Riley attempted to open the general manager's office only to find that the door wouldn't move—it appeared to be blocked on the other side. Upon investigation, she discovered that someone or something had moved three boxes of computer equipment and stacked them against the door. "No one can imagine how this could have happened," she says. "There's no other door and only one high, small window. It took me an hour of inch by inch pushing to get that door open."

The North Annex in the 1913 section is another hot spot. Guests and staff alike report someone running fast down the stairs. A swinging door separates the guest rooms from the hotel meeting room. A staff member was working in that meeting room around 10 a.m. and heard a ruckus. She rushed to the entrance and the swinging door opened in front of her. No one came through and the door swung closed. There was no one in the hallway or stairs and nowhere to hide. But maybe ghosts don't have to hide, they just fade away.

Recently Steve Andrews, a desk clerk spotted a tall gentleman in a tux, top hat, white scarf and cane roaming the halls of the 1928 wing of the building. At his side was a lady in a cream colored gown. Andrews was concerned. The hour

Grande Colonial Hotel historic photograph.

was late and he didn't recognize the couple. Who were they and what were they doing there? He rushed after them, rounding the corner. The hall was empty . . .

At 3 a.m. on the morning of June 6, 2004, a guest in room 122 woke to the sound of running footsteps on the staircase outside her room. Several people ran up and down stomping on each step. A

San Diego Area

door slammed again and again. She lay in bed, covers pulled up, wondering if she dared open the door to see what was going on.

At last the guest got up and peered out.   There was no one to be seen.   The woman was certain that she'd heard multiple heavy footsteps of men running.   The stairs sounded hollow as if there was no carpet on them.   The slamming door she'd heard was   to a meeting room.   At 3 a.m. it seemed unlikely that anything would be taking place there.

The businesses around Grande Colonial Hotel in 1928.

The guest notified the staff and was assured that no one used that room during the wee hours of the morning.   The security staff found nothing unusual.   Nevertheless, the guest was moved to another room so she could sleep easier, away from the noisy ghosts.

The meeting room that figures so often in the hotel's ghost lore is the Sun Room—a favorite for private events because of its sweeping ocean view and cozy fireplace.   However, during WWII, the Sun Room was used as a temporary barracks for single servicemen.   Hardwood floors still exist under the carpet in the North Annex and were uncarpeted during the forties.   The historic battle known as D-Day occurred on June 6, 1944.   Perhaps the spirits of those long ago soldiers were reliving the events of the 60th anniversary of the Normandy Invasion.   Could the running footsteps be the spirits of soldiers preparing to join their comrades in arms across the seas?

Room 220 is also filled with history—and possibly spirits. In 1947, the now world famous La Jolla Playhouse was founded by Gregory Peck, Dorothy McGuire and Mel Ferrer. The enterprise attracted famous stars and aggressive up-and-comers. The guest room most often in demand was 220 with its semi-private entrance that enabled celebrities to keep their private lives . . . well, private.

Mischievous spirits appear to be drawn to the energy. The reception desk has received numerous phone calls from this room and upon answering the call, no one is on the other line. Each time, an employee has been dispatched to the room to make sure everything was okay. Once Steve Andrews saw a figure hiding behind the curtains. As he approached, the curtains fell flat. There was no open window and no breeze to account for the movement.

The 2005 renovation of the hotel and construction of the posh *Nine-Ten* restaurant seemed to literally raise the dead. Restaurant staff would leave pots of broth or sauces simmering overnight for the next day's menus. When they returned the pilot lights would be snuffed out or the stove turned all the way up. During this period Karla Lloyd, a pastry chef, and Matt Rankin, a night auditor, were talking in the kitchen when they observed a frying pan, securely stacked on a rack above them, neatly lift up and set itself down on the counter.

The hotel staff lives with spectral commotion on an ongoing basis. The kitchen and bakery are very active and so is the ladies room. Sometimes doorknobs turn all by themselves. In can get scary. One housekeeper saw faces peering at her. She was spooked enough to switch to the day shift.   Still, she didn't want to leave —and neither apparently do the ghosts.

Grande Hotel Colonial is located at 910 Prospect St.   La Jolla 92037   Tel 858 454-2181 Fax 858 454-5783

San Diego Area

THE FALLBROOK ENTERPRISE

YOU'VE HEARD THE EXPRESSION "DEAD AS YESTERDAY'S newspaper"—but what about a newspaper office?

Staff members of *The Enterprise* in Fallbrook are convinced that their place of employment is haunted.

At first no one wanted to talk about it. Each employee was afraid the others would think she or he was crazy. But the pressure was building and finally somebody had to say something. "Suddenly," Donna Spicer, office manager for the paper's advertising department, recalls "everybody was saying, 'You mean you saw that too?'"

The "that" took a number of forms.

One Sunday Texanna Schaden was alone at *The Enterprise* when she encountered a little girl with long red hair and a full-length dress sitting behind the general manager's desk. Schaden went on about her business for a few minutes and then returned to check on the child and ask where her mother was. There was no child—no mother either—Schaden was alone.

A few Sundays later, another employee asked Schaden if she knew the girl who was sitting at the general manager's desk. When the two women investigated, once again no one was there.

"When you see something and you *know* you saw it and then it's gone—well, it does give you a little chill," Schaden admits.

At first Donna Spicer says the misplaced files and rearranged desk top in the advertising department could be explained away. But then "little mischievous things" started happening two and three times a day. Finally *Enterprise* photographer Dick O'Brien thought it was time to bring in a psychic.

In December of 1988, Alexandra Andrews did a walk-through. The woman who had founded the non-profit Alexandra Institute in San Diego to study psychic phenomena, felt certain that staff members were absolutely right in their assumption. "Something" paranormal was definitely going on at *The Enterprise*.

Then on the night of January 15, 1989 Andrews returned to the newspaper. She wanted to be alone in the building. In one room the psychic "saw" the same shimmering white lights that had previously been reported—*but not to her*—by employees. In another office she detected a presence and the faint scent of roses—hardly the cigar smoke one associates with a newspaper office.

There were fleeting images, Andrews says. The building, she is certain, stood on ground used as a kind of "highway." Perhaps more signficantly, lives had been lost in the area. Andrews was aware of the presence of four entities in *The Enterprise*—a man, woman and two children.

A check with the Fallbrook Historical Society revealed that the land where the newspaper now stands was once owned by a Duthie family who owned a service station and lived in a home behind it. Mr. Duthie died more than fifty years ago in the house. Also dead are his wife and two children. In 1950 the house burned to the ground and was never rebuilt.

The energy that Andrews detected wasn't malicious. "It was almost as if they were still here in order to bring some positive energy to the location," she says. The psychic's theory is an intriguing one. She believes that the newspaper site was no accident.

What better place than a news center to communicate the continuity of the human spirit?

The Enterprise is located on the corner of Elder Street and South Main Avenue in Fallbrook.

San Diego Area

BIBLIOGRAPHY

NORTHERN CALIFORNIA

Boynton, Suzanne. "Ghosts for Guests," *Santa Rosa,* October 25, l990.

Casserly, Joan. "Spirits Served at Local Saloon," *The Sonoma Index-Tribune,* October 31, 1989.

Fein, Julian. "Smoking Out the Ghosts," *Modesto Bee,* December 29, 1981.

Leary, Kevin. "The Ghost of Stinson Beach," *San Francisco Chronicle,* October 29, 1984.

Madlener, Judy. "Following the Gold Rush Trail," *California Living,* March 18, 1979.

Magagnini, Stephen. "The Ghostly Arsonist of the Gold Country," *San Francisco Chronicle,* August 13, 1985.

Sommer, Anna. "That House is Haunted," *The News,* September 16, 1933.

Yarbrough, Carolyn J. "Healdsburg Inn Treats a Guest to a Special Visit," *Los Angeles Times,* March l0, l985.

SAN FRANCISCO AREA

Asbury, Herbert. *The Barbary Coast,* Garden City Publishing Company, Inc., 1933.

Atherton, Gertrude. *Adventures of a Novelist,* Liverright, 1932.

Butler, Phyllis Filiberti. *The Valley of Santa Clara, Historic Buildings, 1792-1920,* The Junior League of San Jose, Inc., 1975.

Carson, Greg. "Split Personality," *Spirit,* April l990.

Chapman, Elizabeth. "I'll Take the Back Road," *Stockton Record,* May 8, 1964.

Conour, Dale. "Peninsula Ghosts," *Peninsula Magazine,* October, 1987.

Dossa, Elizabeth. "The Ghost at Kohl Mansion: Rumor or Reality!", *Hillsborough & Burlingame Boutique & Villager,* October l0, l984.

Dossa, Liz. "Kohl Mansion Restoration Costly, but Complete, *Hillsborough & Burlingame Boutique & Villager,* January l5, l992.

Gleeson, Bill. "Sure-Fire Weekend Getaways," *San Francisco Chronicle,* February ll, l991.

Hatfield, Larry. "Shadows of a doubt," *San Francisco Examiner,* October 31, 1991.

Landmarks Preservation Advisory Board, Revised Case Report, March 20, 1974, The Atherton House.

Landmark Proposal, San Francisco Art Institute.

Leonidas K. Haskell file, California State Historical Society.

McDonald, James M. "Recollections of Early Days in San Francisco," *Harper's Weekly,* October 22, 1859.

Mason, Jack, with Thomas Barfield. *Last Stage for Bolinas,* North Shore Books, 1973.

Montandon, Pat. *The Intruders,* Coward, McCann & Geoghegan, Inc., 1975.

Pack, Robert I. "Rengstorff Mansion Haunted? Whooo Knows?", *Palo Alto Times,* August 10, 1972.

Olmsted, Roger R. *Here Today,* Chronicle Books, 1968.

Peck, Anna Mary. "A Study in Folk Lore," unpublished, 1973.

Saroyan, Wayne A. "'Un-Thanksgiving' on Alcatraz," *San Francisco Chronicle,* November 19, 1989.

Stern, Daniel K. "Guns of Destiny," *Westways,* February 1953.

Svanevik, Michael and Burgett, Shirley. "The Stalking of Charles Frederick Kohl," *Peninsula,* December 1991.

Svanevik, Michael. "Probing Poltergeists on the Peninsula," *The Times,* October 31, 1986.

Svanevik, Michael. "When the Sisters Took Over Kohl Mansion," *The Times,* August 26, 1988.

"The Story of Fort Mason, Historic U. S. Army Post in San Francisco" prepared by the information office, U. S. Army Transportation Terminal Command, Pacific, Fort Mason, December 10, 1960.

Wallace, Kevin. "It's Haunted—But Home," *San Francisco Chronicle,* October 31, 1974.

CENTRAL CALIFORNIA

Blain, Mike. "Paranormal Tendencies," *City on a Hill Press,* April 12, 1991.

Long, Tom. "Brookdale Ghosts Won't Check Out," *Santa Cruz Sentinel,* January 6, 1991.

Morgan, Teri. "New Owners Plan New Beginning for Landmark Brookdale Lodge," *San Jose Mercury,* March 30, 1990.

Rogers, Paul. "Dislodging the Ghosts," *San Jose Mercury,* January 1, 1991.

MOTHER LODE COUNTRY

Centennial Issue—1877-1977, Nevada County Historical Society.

Coats, Rusty. "Patrons Fond of Ghostly Barkeep, *Modesto Bee,* October 31, 1989.

Fein, Julian. "Smoking Out The Ghosts," *Modesto Bee,* December 29, 1981.

Green, George. "The Life and Death of the Willow," *San Francisco Free Paper,* March 1978.

Grieg, Michael. "A Psychic Prober Exorcises Ghosts," *San Francisco Chronicle,* February 4, 1974.

Jerome, Lynn. "Jamestown's Historic Willow Destroyed in $200,000 Blaze," *The Union Democrat,* July 21, 1975.

Jerome, Lynn. "One-Story Willow Rising From Ashes of July Blaze," *The Union Democrat,* October 16, 1975.

Leary, Kevin. "Hotel With Invisible Guests," *San Francisco Chronicle,* October 31, 1987.

SAN DIEGO AREA

Buckley, Marcie. *The Crown City's Brightest Gem,* Hotel del Coronado, 1975.

Crane, Clare. "Jesse Shepard and the Villa Montezuma," *The Journal of San Diego History,* Summer 1970.

Davidson, Winifred. "Hanged for Boat-Stealing," *The San Diego Union,* October 6, 1935.

Davidson, Winifred. "They Blessed This Señorita," *The San Diego Union,* March 17, 1935.

Fitzsimmons, Barbara. "A Grand Ghostly Night," *San Diego Union,* November 25, l987.

Freeman, Don. "The Mocker," *Old West,* Winter, 1973.

Holzer, Hans. *Ghosts of the Golden West,* Ace Books, 1968.

Hugh, Tom and Holly. "Romance Revived at the Horton Grand," *San Francisco Examiner,* June l2, l988l

Perkins, Eloise. "Rancho Jamul Is Where It Happens," *Times-Advocate,* June 22, 1975.

Rice, Edna Taft. *A Clairvoyant Approach to Haunting,* California Parapsychology Foundation, Inc., 1968.

Reading, June A. *The Thomas Whaley House,* Historical Shrine Foundation of San Diego County, 1960.

LOS ANGELES AREA

Hyams, Joe. "Our Haunted House," *Reader's Digest,* November 1966.

Hyams, Joe. "The Day I Gave Up the Ghost," *Saturday Evening Poast,* June 3, 1967.

Moss, Thelma and Schmeidler, Gertrude. "Quantitative Investigation of a 'Haunted House' with Sensitives and a Control Group," *Journal of the American Society for Psychical Research,* Vol. 62, No. 4, October 1968.

Northrop, Marie E. "The Yorba Family Cemetery: California's Oldest," *National Genealogical Society Quarterly, Vol. 57, No. 2, June 1969.*

Central California

Beck, Larry. "Pacheco Pass," The Nirvana Foundation.

Guthertz, Alvin T. "How A Publicity Stunt Turned Up A Ghost." *Psychic World,* September 1976.

Rambo, Ralph. *Lady of Mystery,* The Rosicrucian Press, 1967.

Reinstedt, Randall A. *Ghosts, Bandits & Legends of Old Monterey,* Ghost Town Publications, 1974.

Taff, B. E. "Stalking the Elusive Spectre," *Probe,* October 1973.

Taff, Barry E. and Gaynor, Kerry. "A New Poltergeist Effect," *Theta, A Journal for Research on the Question of Survival After Death,* Vol. 4, No. 2, Spring 1976.

Taff, Barry E. and Gaynor, Kerry. "Another Wild Ghost Chase?: No, One Hell of a Haunt," The Neuropsychiatric Institute, UCLA Center for the Health Sciences.

Vance, Adrian. "UCLA Group Uses Camera To Hunt Ghosts," *Popular Photography,* May 1976.

MISCELLANEOUS

Bungess, Michelle. "West Coast Spirits," *Alaska Airlines Magazine,* May 1989.

Caughey, John W. *California,* Prentice-Hall, 1953.

Haining, Peter. *Ghosts,* Macmillian Publishing Co., inc. 1975.

Hoover, Mildred Brooke; Rensch, Ethel; Rensch, Hero. *Historic Spots in California,* Stanford University Press, 1966.

Marinacci, Mike. *Mysterious California,* Panpipes Press, 1988.

Mitchell, Edgar. *Psychic Explorations, a Challenge to Science,* Putnam, 1974.

Nava, Julian and Barger, Bob. *California,* Glencoe Press, 1976.

Newcomb, Rexford. *The Old Missions and Historic Homes of California,* J. B. Lippincott Company, 1925.

Pelton, Charles C. *Psychic Photography Finally Explored,* Pelton Publications, Pinole, CA 1990.

Pomada, Elizabeth and Larsen, Michael. *The Painted Ladies Guide to Victorian California. Dutton Studio Books,* 1991.

INDEX

ABOUT THE AUTHOR

Antoinette May, an author-journalist, lectures on parapsychology at universities and colleges. She is a former newspaper editor with a lifelong interest in the occult. As a psychic researcher whose work has been featured on numerous TV documentaries such as *In Search Of* and *The World of People*. May has devoted many years to the study of ghosts. *Adventures of a Psychic* was 42 weeks on the *New York Times* best seller list. Her website is antoinettemay.com.

Other books by Antoinette May include—

Pilate's Wife

The Yucatan: A Guide to the Land of Maya Mysteries

Mexico for Lovers

Witness to War

The Annotated Ramona

Psychic Women

Helen Hunt Jackson: A Lonely Voice of Conscience

Different Drummers

Passionate Pilgrim

The Adventures of a Psychic (originally *My Guide, Myself*)